System Aids in
Constructing Consultation Programs

Computer Science:
Artificial Intelligence, No. 11

Harold S. Stone, Series Editor

President, The Interfactor, Inc.

Other Titles in This Series

System Aids in
Constructing Consultation Programs

by
William J. van Melle

UMI RESEARCH PRESS
Ann Arbor, Michigan

Produced and distributed by
UMI Research Press
an imprint of
University Microfilms International
Ann Arbor, Michigan 48106

Library of Congress Cataloging in Publication Data

van Melle, William J. (William James)
System aids in constructing consultation programs.

(Computer science. Artificial intelligence ; no. 11)
Revision of thesis—Stanford University, 1980.
Bibliography: p.
Includes index.
1. Expert system (Computer science) I. Title.
II. Series.

QA76.9.E96V36   1981   001.64'25   81-13132
ISBN 0-8357-1232-X   AACR2

Contents

List of Figures

Acknowledgments

Portions of the EMYCIN system draw heavily on earlier MYCIN work. While responsibility for the bulk of the actual code in the present system is mine, most of the features described in Chapter 2 (with the exception of antecedent rules) originated with other members of the MYCIN project. Ted Shortliffe wrote the original MYCIN program, from which the basic rule representation, associative triples, and CF mechanism arose, together with the basic backward-chaining rule interpreter. Randy Davis is responsible for Preview, Unitypath, Metarules, and the **HOW/WHY** explanation facility. Several people from Ted onward have had a hand in the QA module, but the bulk of the work has been by Carli Scott, including the separation of domain-specific from domain-independent code needed to make the QA module a functioning part of EMYCIN. Carli has also taken active part in other EMYCIN developments, notably the recent adaptation of portions of Randy's TEIRESIAS progam that are used in knowledge base debugging.

I would like to thank Bruce Buchanan for numerous helpful comments, suggestions, and enlightening discussions. His continual concern for my work has been most encouraging, and his aid was invaluable in getting this thesis to finally emerge.

I would also like to thank Randy Davis, Doug Lenat, and Gio Wiederhold. Thanks also to Carli Scott, Jim Bennett, and Jan Clayton for their comments on earlier drafts of this study, and to Jan Aikins, Larry Fagan, and Bill Clancey for miscellaneous discussion.

Finally, I would like to thank my friends for their moral support and encouragement through the rough moments.

This work was supported in part by the National Science Foundation (grants MCS 77-02712 and MCS-7903753) and the Defense Advance Research Projects Agency (contract MDA 903-77-C-0302).

1

Introduction

Much current work in artificial intelligence focuses on computer programs that aid scientists with complex reasoning tasks. Recent work has indicated that one key to the creation of intelligent systems is the incorporation of large amounts of task-specific knowledge. Building such "knowledge-based" or "expert" systems from scratch can be very time-consuming, however, which suggests the need for general tools to aid the construction of knowledge-based systems.

This study demonstrates an effective domain-independent framework for constructing one class of expert programs: rule-based consultants. The system, called EMYCIN,[1] is based on the domain-independent core of the MYCIN program [Shortliffe 76]. Domain knowledge is represented in EMYCIN primarily as production rules, which are applied by a goal-directed backward-chaining control structure. Rules and consultation data may have associated measures of certainty, and incomplete data are allowed. The system includes an explanation facility that can display the line of reasoning followed by the consultation program, or answer questions from the user about the contents of its knowledge base. Other built-in human-engineering features allow the system architect to produce, with a minimum of effort, a consultation program that is pleasing in appearance to the user.

1.1 The Task

EMYCIN is used to construct a *consultation program*, by which we mean a program that offers advice on problems within its domain of expertise. The consultation program elicits information relevant to the case by asking questions. It then applies its knowledge to the specific facts of the case and informs the user of its conclusions. The user is free to ask the program questions about its reasoning in order to better understand or validate the advice given.

There are really two "users" of EMYCIN, as depicted in Figure 1-1.

The *system designer* or *expert*[2] interacts with EMYCIN to produce a *knowledge base* for the domain. EMYCIN then interprets this knowledge base to provide advice to the *client* or *consultation user*. Thus the "consultation program" seen by the client consists of EMYCIN 's consultation driver together with the knowledge base.

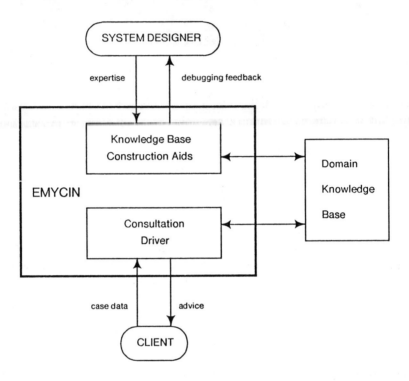

Figure 1-1. The major roles of EMYCIN: acquiring a knowledge base from the system designer, and interpreting that knowledge base to provide advice to a client.

Excerpts from a sample consultation follow. The program demonstrated here is CLOT [Bennett 80]; it requests clinical evidence regarding an episode of bleeding, facts from the patient's general medical history, and the results of a battery of coagulation screening tests. From these data the program infers the presence and type of coagulation defect (if any) in the patient and then proceeds to make a refined diagnosis for any particular enzymatic deficiency or platelet defect. The program was built using EMYCIN, but this brief example shows only a client's interaction with the consultation driver on a particular case after the preliminary knowledge base had been constructed and (largely) debugged.

In this, as in all subsequent examples, user input appears in **BOLD ITALICS** (always following the double-asterisk prompt in this excerpt), while annotations are set off in *light italics*; `all other text` is printed by the program.

```
--------PATIENT-1--------
```
The program first gathers general patient data.

```
1) Name:
** FRED
2) Age:
** 23
3) Sex:
** MALE
4) Race:
** CAUCASIAN
```

The client need not type long answers; typing Escape causes EMYCIN to complete a partial answer from its list of expected responses.

```
5) Please indicate your reason(s) for requesting this consultation:
** BLEEDING-HISTORY
```
Given the reason for the consultation, the program now asks for details of the latest bleeding episode.

```
6) What type of bleeding describes Fred's most recent episode of
   bleeding?
** HEMMARTHROSIS
=HEMARTHROSIS
```
Program performs spelling correction on erroneous inputs.

```
7) Is there a history of a genetic bleeding disorder in Fred's
   family?
** Y

8) Was the onset of the bleeding immediate or delayed?
** IMMEDIATE
```
Following are results from a battery of lab tests.[3]

```
9) Pt:
** 14
10) Ptt:
** 30
11) Pc:
** 200000
12) Bt:
** 5
13 Tt:
** 16
14) Fsf:
** NORMAL
```

The program infers what it can about the patient's coagulative disorder, and displays its findings to the client. The numbers in parentheses indicate relative certainty in the conclusions, on a scale of 0 to 1.

The final blood disorders of Fred are as follows:

> COAGULATION-DEFECT (.97).
> PLATELET-VASCULAR-DEFECT (.5).

There is a consistent estimation of the blood defect of Fred (.68).

The blood coagulation diagnoses of Fred are as follows:

> The patient has a factor VII deficiency (.97).

> *"Factor VII" denotes a particular enzymatic deficiency.*

1.2 Applications

Several consultation systems have been written in EMYCIN. All but the most recent of these were developed in parallel with EMYCIN, and thus served to focus attention on certain features and shortcomings of the program to guide in its development. Their description here is intended to provide some indication of the range of potential applications of EMYCIN.

1.2.1 MYCIN

The original MYCIN program provides advice on the diagnosis of and therapy for infectious diseases. MYCIN is now implemented in EMYCIN, but its knowledge base was largely constructed before the development of EMYCIN. Results of formal evaluations of MYCIN's competence in the domains of bacteremia (bacterial infections in the blood) and meningitis indicate that MYCIN's performance in these areas has begun to approach that of medical specialists [Yu 79a], [Yu 79b].

1.2.2 PUFF

The PUFF program [Kunz 78] performs interpretation of measurements from the pulmonary function laboratory. PUFF's knowledge base was constructed using an early version of EMYCIN; the system designers were Stanford computer scientists who had previous experience with MYCIN, collaborating with a pulmonary physiologist and biomedical engineers. The data from over 100 cases were used to create some 60 rules diagnosing the presence of pulmonary disease. The rules are used to create a complete report including the input measurements, other patient data, and the measurement interpretation.

The PUFF rule set was expanded and converted into a BASIC program, which runs on a PDP-11 at Pacific Medical Center in San Francisco. The system is used regularly by the pulmonary function laboratory there. Its reports are reviewed by a staff physician before being entered into the patient's record; most reports (95%) are accepted without change.

1.2.3 HEADMED

The HEADMED program [Heiser 78] is an application of EMYCIN to clinical psychopharmacology. The system diagnoses a range of psychiatric disorders and recommends drug treatment when indicated.

1.2.4 SACON

As a stronger test of domain independence, EMYCIN was applied to the non-medical domain of structural analysis. SACON (structural analysis consultation) [Bennett 78] provides advice to a structural engineer regarding the use of a large structural analysis program called MARC. The MARC program uses finite-element analysis techniques to simulate the mechanical behavior of objects. The engineer typically knows what she wants the MARC program to do, e.g., examine the behavior of a specific structure under expected loading conditions, but does not know how the simulation program should be set up to do it. The goal of the SACON program is to recommend an analysis strategy; this advice can then be used to direct the MARC user in the choice of specific input data, numerical methods, and material properties.

The performance of the SACON program matches that of a human consultant for the limited domain of structural analysis problems that was initially selected. To bring the SACON program to its present level of performance, about two man-months of the experts' time were required to explicate their task as consultants and formulate the knowledge base, and about the same amount of time to implement and test the rules in a preliminary version of EMYCIN.

1.2.5 CLOT

A recent application of EMYCIN is CLOT [Bennett 80], an experimental system designed to diagnose disorders of the blood coagulation system of patients. These diagnoses can be used by a physician to estimate the severity and cause of a particular episode of bleeding, evaluate the effects of various anti-coagulation therapies on a patient, or estimate the pre-operative risk of a patient having serious bleeding problems during surgery.

CLOT was constructed as a joint effort by James Bennett at Stanford and David Goldman, a medical student at the University of Missouri. Following approximately ten hours of discussion about the contents of the knowledge base, they entered and debugged in another ten hours a preliminary knowledge base of some sixty rules using EMYCIN.[4]

1.3 Historical Background

Some of the earliest work in artificial intelligence centered around attempts to create generalized problem solvers. Work on programs like GPS [Newell 72] and theorem proving [Nilsson 71], for instance, was inspired by the apparent generality of human intelligence and motivated by the desire to develop a single program applicable to many problems. While this early work demonstrated the utility of many general-purpose techniques (such as problem decomposition into subgoals and heuristic search in its many forms), these techniques alone did not offer sufficient power for high performance in complex domains.

Recent work has instead focused on the incorporation of large amounts of task-specific knowledge in what have been called "knowledge-based" systems. Rather than non-specific problem solving power, knowledge-based systems have emphasized high performance based on the accumulation of large amounts of knowledge about a single domain. Some examples to date include efforts at symbolic manipulation of algebraic expressions [Macsyma 74], chemical inference [Buchanan 78], and medical consultations [Pople 77], [Shortliffe 76].

While these systems display an expert level of performance, each is powerful in only a very narrow domain. In addition, assembling the knowledge base and constructing a working program for such domains is a difficult, continuous task that has often extended over several years. However, one of these systems, MYCIN, included in its design the goal of keeping the domain knowledge well separated from the program that manipulates the knowledge.[5] Thus, while MYCIN itself is specific to the domain of infectious diseases and thus not at all general, the basic rule methodology provided a foundation for a more general rule-based system.

1.3.1 Development of EMYCIN

Actually achieving the desired generality took somewhat longer. Despite the stated design goal, there was much code in MYCIN that referred to specific aspects of the infectious disease domain. These ranged from the simple cases of strings and other quoted text referring to "the patient" (these were changed to refer to variable strings, or more generally to "the case"), to instances of actual domain knowledge in the code, especially in the question answering (QA) module. In some cases this knowledge was reformulated into rules, while other instances became domain-specific "hooks" (e.g., a parsing hook in the QA module to handle questions about the therapy algorithm).

The system resulting from the extraction of all the infectious-disease knowledge had one glaring deficiency: it emphasized interpreting an existing knowledge base and did not facilitate constructing the initial knowledge base in a new domain. MYCIN was a large system that changed only slowly over time, whereas a large part of the effort in creating a consultant in a new domain goes into the initial construction of the knowledge base, which requires the entry and debugging of many rules and other structures of the domain. More than half of the development effort of EMYCIN has focused on speedy and accurate knowledge aquisition.

Once a consultation program is built, however, it becomes important that it perform efficiently; this is most noticeable in such large programs as MYCIN. Production rules, while convenient in their modularity, are not the best representation for speedy interpretation. We have thus developed a "rule compiler" for EMYCIN that transforms a program's production rules into a decision tree, eliminating the redundant computation inherent in a rule interpreter, and compiles the resulting tree into machine code. The program can thereby use an efficient deductive mechanism for running the actual consultation, while the flexible rule format remains available for acquisition, explanation, and debugging.

With the development of EMYCIN we have now come full circle to GPS's philosophy of separating the deductive mechanism from the problem-specific knowledge; however, EMYCIN's extensive user facilities make it a much more accessible environment for producing expert systems than the earlier programs.

1.4   Related Work

1.4.1   Production Systems

Production systems were originally proposed by Post [Post 43] as a general computational mechanism, equivalent in power to a Turing machine. They have since seen extensive use in the study of formal grammars, compilers, and control theory. Several string-manipulation languages have been written in the style of production systems, the best known of which is perhaps SNOBOL. For a good overview of production systems, see [Davis 77b].

"Pure" production systems (consisting of a simple recognize-act cycle) such as PSG [Newell 73] have been used for modeling cognitive processes. The amount of information contained in a single rule is small; each rule performs low-level primitive operations on tokens in the working memory (which may or may not be viewed as representing human short- or long-term memory). OPS [Forgy 79b], the successor to PSG, drops PSG's convention of a fixed rule order, using instead more sophisticated *conflict resolution* schemes to determine which of several potentially applicable productions to try next (select a specific production over a more general one, select a production matching more recent data, etc.; see [McDermott 78] for discussion).

Work in the performance-oriented, expert systems, on the other hand, has tended to use production rules with higher-level primitives, and are not concerned with any equivalence between the control mechanisms and how humans perform a task. DENDRAL [Buchanan 78] has rules expressed in terms of chemical bond structures, with primitives such as breaking a bond. MYCIN's rules use concepts such as a patient's symptoms and results of lab tests.

1.4.2   Other Knowledge-Based Systems Work

EXPERT [Weiss 79] is another example of a domain-independent framework evolved from a specific medical application—it is a system for writing medical consultants, based on the CASNET program [Weiss 78]. A domain model in EXPERT consists primarily of a set of *findings* (input data), a set of *hypotheses* (conclusions to be inferred by the system) structured into a taxonomic classification scheme, and a collection of rules that describe the logical relationships between findings and/or hypotheses. Inference is performed both by firing rules and by propagating hypothesis weights through the causal taxonomic network. The rules are fired in a data-driven fashion, but questions asked of the user are selected by a goal-oriented approach: the system seeks rules that bear most strongly on the current hypothesis and chooses from one of those rules an unasked finding of minimum cost and maximum benefit.

PROSPECTOR [Duda 78] is a knowledge-based consultant for aiding geologists in certain mineral exploration problems. Domain knowledge is represented in an *inference network*; the nodes are assertions about entities in the domain, which may be true or false (with some probability) in any particular case, and the arcs are inference rules that indicate how the likelihood of one assertion affects the likelihood of another. Domain entities are also arranged in a taxonomic network, allowing the system to do some reasoning by observing subset/superset relations between assertions. The consultation dialogue is mixed-initiative, allowing the user to volunteer information in simple statements, or to answer questions posed by the system. The system propagates the user's initial assertions through the inference network, and on that basis selects one of its "models" to explore further. Rules are selected in a backward-chaining fashion, but rather than searching depth-first (trying all rules potentially relevant to the current goal before going on), the system instead selects at each step the rule that could potentially contribute the most information to the current hypothesis.[6]

1.5   Overview of the Research

Chapter 2 describes the basic architecture of EMYCIN: the knowledge representation used, how it is applied, and generally what makes up the consultation program. Much of this description will be familiar to those already acquainted with the MYCIN literature, but Section 2.6 goes into more detail than usually found elsewhere. The chapter closes with a description of the applications programs in terms of the architectural features.

The remainder of the research is presented from the perspective of the potential system architect rather than the user of the resulting consultation program. Chapter 3 gives an extended example of how one might build a consultant for a new domain. Chapter 4 goes behind the scenes of the example to describe in some detail the knowledge acquisition facilities and other aspects of the EMYCIN environment in which the consultant is being built. Chapter 5 is devoted to a description of the rule compiler. Finally, Chapter 6 discusses the assumptions and limitations inherent in the EMYCIN approach.

1.6   Implementation Notes

EMYCIN was developed on the SUMEX-AIM computer system at Stanford. EMYCIN is written in INTERLISP and runs on a DEC PDP-10 or -20 under the TENEX or TOPS20 operating systems. The current implementation of EMYCIN uses about 45K words of resident memory and an additional 80K of swapped code space. The version of INTERLISP in which it is embedded occupies about 130K of resident memory, leaving approximately 80K free for the domain knowledge base and the dynamic data structures built up during a consultation. Of the knowledge bases mentioned, only MYCIN's approaches the available limits. We are considering further jettisoning unused INTERLISP modules to achieve a more spacious environment.

A manual detailing the operation of the system for the prospective system designer is available [van Melle 80].

2

System Architecture

This chapter describes the basic knowledge representation in EMYCIN, the control structure of EMYCIN's consultation driver, and how the resulting consultation program appears to its user. Much of this material repeats previous reports on the MYCIN program [Shortliffe 76], [Davis 77a], and thus may be familiar to those readers already acquainted with the MYCIN literature; Section 2.6, however, covers some less-publicized details of the system architecture for those wishing a more complete picture of the EMYCIN architecture. Some of that detail is relevant to later sections of the research (Chapters 4 and 5).

2.1 Knowledge Organization

2.1.1 Facts

Knowledge in EMYCIN is represented in terms of production rules operating on associative (attribute-object-value) triples. The *objects* are called *contexts*, and are actual or conceptual entities in the domain of the consultation. The *attributes* in EMYCIN are called *parameters*; they are characteristics of the objects. Questions asked and inferences made during the consultation attempt to fill in the *values* for relevant attributes of the objects.

To represent the uncertainty of data or competing hypotheses, attached to each triple is a *certainty factor* (CF), a number between −1 and 1 indicating the strength of the belief in that fact. A CF of 1 represents total certainty, while a CF of −1 represents certainty in the negation of the fact. While certainty factors are not conditional probabilities, they are informally based in probability theory (see [Shortliffe 75] for details).

Some triples from the structural analysis domain (SACON) might be

	parameter		context		value (CF)
(a)	COMPOSITION	*of*	SUB-STRUCTURE-2	*is*	CONCRETE (1.0)
(b)	GEOMETRY	*of*	SUB-STRUCTURE-2	*is*	PLANAR (-1.0)
(c)	TIME-DEPENDENT	*of*	STRUCTURE-24	*is*	YES (1.0)

in other words, (a) the composition of the second sub-structure is concrete, (b) the geometry of the second sub-structure is *not* planar, and (c) there are time-dependent terms in the equilibrium equations of Structure 24. Multiple values for a single context and parameter are permitted when the CF's are less than unity; e.g., alternative hypotheses for the identity of an organism in MYCIN might be[1]

(d)	IDENTITY	*of*	ORGANISM-1	*is*	PSEUDOMONAS (.8)
(e)	IDENTITY	*of*	ORGANISM-1	*is*	E.COLI (.15),

indicating (d) the identity of Organism 1 is probably Pseudomonas, but (e) there is some evidence to believe it is E. coli.[2]

2.1.2 Rules

The system reasons about its domain using knowledge encoded as *production rules*:

if *premise* **then** *action*.

Each rule has a *premise*, which is a conjunction of predicates over fact triples in the knowledge base. If the premise is true, the conclusion in the *action* part of the rule is drawn, updating one or more fact triples in the knowledge base. If the premise is known with less than certainty, the strength of the conclusion is modified accordingly (see [Shortliffe 75]). Figure 2-1 shows typical rules from the domains of infectious diseases and structural analysis. The English version of the rule is shown first; this is the form in which the user of the consultation program sees the rule. The second version is the internal LISP form manipulated by the program; the English version is generated automatically from the LISP form on demand.

The predicates are simple LISP functions operating on associative triples. **$AND**, the multivalued analogue of the Boolean **and** function, performs a minimization operation on CF's. The body of the rule is actually an executable piece of LISP code, and "evaluating" the premise or action of a rule (Section 2.2) entails little more than applying the LISP function EVAL.

MYCIN's Rule 35

```
If:    1) the gram stain of the organism is gram negative, and
       2) the morphology of the organism is rod, and
       3) the aerobicity of the organism is anaerobic,
Then:  There is suggestive evidence (.6) that the identity
       of the organism is Bacteroides.

       PREMISE:  ($AND (SAME CNTXT GRAM GRAMNEG)
                       (SAME CNTXT MORPH ROD)
                       (SAME CNTXT AIR ANAEROBIC))
       ACTION:   (CONCLUDE CNTXT IDENT BACTEROIDES TALLY 600)³
```

SACON's Rule 68

```
If:    1) The material composing the sub-structure is one of
          the metals,
       2) The analysis error (in percent) that is tolerable is
          less than 5,
       3) The non-dimensional stress of the sub-structure is
          greater than .5, and
       4) The number of cycles the loading is to be applied is
          greater than 10000
Then:  Fatigue is one of the stress behaviour phenomena in the
       sub-structure.

       PREMISE:  ($AND (SAME CNTXT COMPOSITION (LISTOF METALS))
                       (LESSP* (VAL1 CNTXT ERROR)
                               5)
                       (GREATERP* (VAL1 CNTXT ND-STRESS)
                                  .5)
                       (GREATERP* (VAL1 CNTXT CYCLES)
                                  10000))
       ACTION:   (CONCLUDE CNTXT SS-STRESS FATIGUE TALLY 1000)
```

Figure 2-1. Sample rules from two EMYCIN domains, showing
both the pseudo-English and LISP forms.

2.2 Application of Rules—the Rule Interpreter

The control structure is primarily a goal-directed backward-chaining of
rules. At any given time, EMYCIN is working toward the goal of estab-
lishing the value of some parameter of a context; this operation is termed
tracing the parameter. To this end, the system retrieves the (precomputed)
list of rules whose conclusions bear on the goal. SACON's Rule 68 above,
for example, would be one of the rules retrieved in the attempt to determine the stress of a sub-structure. Then for each rule in the list, EMYCIN
evaluates the premise; if true, it makes the conclusion indicated in the
action. The order of the rules in the list is assumed to be arbitrary,[4] and
all the rules are applied unless one of them succeeds and concludes the

value of the parameter with certainty (in which case the remaining rules are superfluous).

In the course of evaluating the premise of one of the rules, some clause might not yet be known, i.e., the context/parameter pair tested in the clause has not yet been traced. In this case, EMYCIN suspends interpretation of the rule while it satisfies the subgoal of finding out (tracing) the unknown parameter; this may in turn cause other rules to be invoked.

Questions are asked during the consultation when the rules fail to deduce the necessary information (or there are no rules at all to conclude it). If the client cannot supply the requested information, it remains unknown, and rules that require it will fail. Thus, applying the rules sets up goals, which in turn invoke other rules (i.e., the rules "chain backward" from the top-level goal to the low-level data); it is the attempt to achieve each goal that drives the consultation. The whole process begins by tracing the top-level "goal" parameter, generally the "result" of the consultation program (e.g., a diagnosis or recommendation). The system's inference procedure can be viewed roughly as the depth-first exploration of an **AND/OR** goal tree, where each **AND** node corresponds to a rule (*all* of the rule's premise clauses must be satisfied) and the **OR** nodes are the parameters tested in each rule (*any* one or more of the rules for a parameter may conclude its value). The root of the tree is the **OR** node consisting of the top-level goal.[5]

Note that this control structure attempts to ask only "relevant" questions. That is, a question is asked only if the information (the value of the parameter) is needed by some rule under consideration, and the rule is only being tried because it is relevant to some goal the system is trying to achieve. Thus, the questions asked, and the order in which they are asked, may vary from case to case; this contrasts with consultants that have a static set of questions, independent of the data actually gathered. The rules themselves need not be concerned with whether the parameter is already known or still needs to be traced; a parameter of a context is traced exactly once (the first time it is needed), and thereafter any reference to it returns the same value.

This control structure was also designed to be able to deal gracefully with incomplete information. If the user is unable to supply some piece of data, the rules that need the data will fail and make no conclusion. The system will thus make conclusions based on less information. Similarly, if the system has inadequate rules (or none at all) for concluding some parameter, it may ask the user for the value. When too many items of information are missing, of course, the system will be unable to offer sound advice.

2.3   Usefulness of the Rule Representation

There are many advantages in having rules as the primary representation of knowledge. Since each rule is intended to be a single "chunk" of information, the knowledge base is inherently modular, making it relatively easy to update. Individual rules can be added, deleted, or modified without drastically affecting the overall performance of the system. The rules are also a convenient unit for explanation purposes, as a single step in the reasoning process can be meaningfully explained by citing the rule used.

The simple, stylized nature of the rules is also useful. The pseudo-English translation of a LISP rule, for example, is made possible by the association of a translation pattern with each predicate function, indicating the logical roles of the function's arguments.

While the syntax of rules permits the use of any LISP functions, there is a small set of standard functions that are used in the vast majority of the rules. The system contains information about the use of these predicates and functions in the form of function *templates*. For example, the predicate **SAME** is described as follows:

function template: **(SAME CNTXT PARM VALUE)**
sample function call: **(SAME CNTXT SITE BLOOD)**.

The system can use these templates to "read" its own rules. For example, the template shown here contains the standard symbols **CNTXT**, **PARM**, and **VALUE**, indicating the components of the associative triple that **SAME** tests. If the clause above appears in the premise of a given rule, the system can determine that the rule needs to know the site of the culture, and in particular that it tests whether the culture site is blood. When asked to display rules that are relevant to blood cultures, the system will be able to select that rule.

One fundamental use of templates is the automatic generation of the lists of rules that conclude about each parameter, used by the rule interpreter when tracing a parameter (Section 2.2). The system scans the **ACTION** of each rule in the knowledge base, matching each clause against the template for the function it uses, and adding the rule to the lists of the appropriate parameter(s).

2.4   The Context Tree

The objects discussed in an EMYCIN consultation are termed *contexts*. A domain may have several *types* of contexts, and a consultation typically has multiple instances of each type. The rules, however, mention only the type of a context, without regard to how many instances of it there are in a particular consultation, or which one is being discussed; thus, contexts function as the primary form of a "variable" in EMYCIN rules[6]

The contexts in a particular consultation are organized into what is termed the *context tree*. Except for the root context, there may be multiple instances of each type of context. The links between contexts are made automatically according to a static, predefined hierarchy of the context types. A context tree from a typical infectious disease consultation is shown in Figure 2-2.

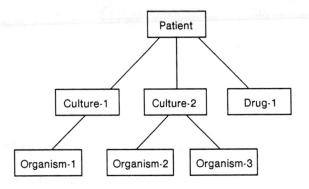

Figure 2-2. Sample context tree from a MYCIN consultation.

The context tree serves two main purposes. First, it indicates the explicit relationships among objects in the consultation, providing a sort of "binding" or "inheritance" mechanism: one rule can refer to parameters of more than one context. For example, the system will automatically make the correct associations when a rule refers to both the site of a culture and the identity of the organism growing out of that culture. Second, it provides a means of structuring the consultation. EMYCIN starts the consultation by setting up the root of the tree and from there setting up as needed the other nodes of the tree, inquiring about basic information at each node (e.g., age of the patient, site and date of the culture). The consultation thus is more structured than it would be if questions were ordered only by the system's logical requirements for information.

In some simple domains the context tree may be degenerate—there is only one node (the root), and all of the system parameters apply to that node.

2.5   Explanation Capability

EMYCIN's *explanation program* allows the user to interrogate the system's knowledge, either to find out about inferences made (or not made) during a particular consultation or to examine the static knowledge base in general, independent of any specific consultation.

During the consultation, EMYCIN can offer explanations of the current, past, and likely future lines of reasoning. If the motivation for any question that the program asks is unclear, the client may temporarily put off answering and instead inquire why the information is needed. Since each question is asked during the attempt to evaluate some rule, a first approximation at an answer is simply to display the rule currently under consideration. The program can also explain what reasoning led to the current point, and what use might later be made of the information being requested. This is made possible by examining records left by the rule interpreter, and by reading the rules in the knowledge base to determine which are relevant. This form of explanation requires no language understanding on the part of the program; it is invoked by simple commands from the client ("**WHY**" and "**HOW**") [Davis 76].

The following example from MYCIN shows the **WHY** command being used to ascend the current reasoning chain. Each successive **WHY** asks why the subgoal of the previous response is being sought; the answer is, of course, the rule whose premise needs the subgoal. Eventually, **WHY** reaches the top of the subgoal tree, i.e., the main goal of the consultation. The client can also ask **HOW** any of the clauses mentioned in the rules displayed by **WHY** are known or will be found out. The two commands together allow the client to step through any path in the system's reasoning that is "reachable" from the current state.

Figure 2-3. Using WHY in the MYCIN domain to ascend the subgoal tree in order to understand the current line of reasoning in a specific consultation, and using HOW to understand the reasoning that led to the facts already known.

```
34) Was penicillinase added to this blood culture (CULTURE-1)?
** WHY

[i.e. WHY is it important to determine whether penicillinase was
      added to CULTURE-1?]

[3.0] This will aid in determining whether ORGANISM-1 is a
      contaminant.
   It has already been established that
      [3.1] the site of CULTURE-1 is blood, and
      [3.2] the gram stain of ORGANISM-1 is grampos
```

Therefore, if
   [3.3] penicillinase was added to this blood culture
then
   there is weakly suggestive evidence (.4) that ORGANISM-1 is a
     contaminant
[RULE039]

   ** WHY

[i.e. WHY is it important to determine whether ORGANISM-1 is a
   contaminant?]

[4.0] ... in order to determine whether there is significant disease
associated with this occurrence of ORGANISM-1.
  It has already been established that
   [4.1] this blood culture was taken from a sterile source
Therefore, if
   [4.2] ORGANISM-1 is not a contaminant
then
   there is strongly suggestive evidence (.9) that there is
   significant disease associated with this occurrence of ORGANISM-1
[RULE032]

   ** WHY

[i.e. WHY is it important to determine whether there is significant
   disease associated with this occurrence of ORGANISM-1?]

[5.0] ... in order to determine the organisms which require therapy.
  It has already been established that
   [5.1] the infection is known, and
   [5.2] the identity of ORGANISM-1 is known
Therefore, if
   [5.3] there is significant disease associated with this
     occurrence of ORGANISM-1
then
   ORGANISM-1 is one of the organisms which require therapy
[RULE090]

   ** HOW 5.2
[i.e. HOW was it established that the identity of ORGANISM-1 is
   known?]

Question 9 was asked, but you weren't sure; so the following was used:

  [5.5] RULE084 was used to conclude that the identity of ORGANISM-1
    is Streptococcus-group-a (.29).

Another form of explanation is available via the *question answering (QA) module*, which is automatically invoked after the consultation has ended, and which can also be entered during the consultation to answer questions other than the specialized **WHY/HOW** described above. The QA module accepts simple English-language questions (a) dealing with any conclusion drawn during the consultation, or (b) about the domain in general. The level of explanation is again that of the rules, presumably comprehensible to anyone familiar with the domain, even if not familiar with the intricacies of the EMYCIN system. The questions are parsed by pattern matching and keyword lookup, using a dictionary that defines the vocabulary of the domain. EMYCIN automatically constructs the dictionary from the phrases used in defining the contexts and parameters of the domain; the system designer may refine this preliminary dictionary to add synonyms or better tune QA's parsing. The QA module is described in much more detail elsewhere [Scott 77]. Examples of the sorts of questions one can ask in the QA module are shown in Figures 2-4 and 2-5.

Figure 2-4. General questions about the MYCIN and SACON domains.

```
** IS BACTEROIDES AEROBIC?

No, the aerobicity of Bacteroides is anaerobic.

** WHAT ORGANISMS ARE LIKELY TO BE FOUND IN THE THROAT?
The likely pathogens associated with throat are:  DIPLOCOCCUS-
    PNEUMONIAE, STREPTOCOCCUS-GROUP-A, NEISSERIA-MENINGITIDIS.

                   _____


** HOW DO YOU USE THE GEOMETRY OF A SUB-STRUCTURE?
The following rules use:
     the geometry of the sub-structure

53, 48, 102, 101, 100

The parameters concluded by these rules are:
     the shape of the sub-structure
     the analysis recommendations to be considered when preparing
         the structure for modelling

Which of the rules do you wish to see?
     ** 53

RULE053
-------
```

```
If:   1) Buckling is one of the deflection phenomena in the
         structure, and
      2) You have examined the sub-structures, and have found one
         for which the geometry of this sub-structure is curved
Then:   The following is one of the analysis recommendations to be
        considered when preparing the structure for modelling:
        Buckling estimates should be based on incremental load
        analysis.
```

Figure 2-5. Examples of questions about a particular MYCIN consultation.

** *IS ORGANISM-1 A STREPTOCOCCUS?*

```
No.   The identity of ORGANISM-1 is E.coli (.74) Bacteroides (.7)
      Klebsiella-pneumoniae (.4) Pseudomonas-aeruginosa (.??)
      Enterobacter ( ?1) Proteus-non-mirabilis (.19) Serratia (.03)
      Salmonella (.02)
```

** *WHY DID YOU RULE OUT STREPTOCOCCUS AS A POSSIBILITY FOR ORGANISM-1?*

```
RULE033 could have been used to determine that the identity of
ORGANISM-1 is Streptococcus. However, clause 2 of rule033 ["the
morphology of the organism is coccus"] was already known to be
false for ORGANISM-1, so the rule was never tried.
```

2.6   Elaboration on the Basic Architecture

The features discussed below fall into categories of (a) ways by which the system designer can alter the flow of control (the order in which questions are asked, rules tried, parameters traced), (b) system mechanisms for better focusing the deductive mechanism, and (c) language devices for increasing the expressive power of the rules and data structures.

2.6.1   Altering the Control Flow

The simple method of backchaining rules and asking questions when the rules fail to deduce needed information, while logically sufficient, does not always satisfy other constraints, such as asking questions in a "sensible" order. EMYCIN provides several features that allow the system designer to exercise greater control over the rule interpreter's behavior.

2.6.1.1 ASKFIRST parameters.   Ordinarily when tracing a parameter, EMYCIN attempts to deduce the parameter by using rules, and failing that, asks the client.[7] The designer may mark parameters instead as information likely to be readily available from the client;[8] in this case the

system asks first, and only tries rules if the client cannot supply the information.

By tagging a parameter **ASKFIRST**, the designer saves the interpreter from needlessly trying rules when the client is likely to know, and can easily supply, the parameter's value. This allows the designer to incorporate rules that deduce the parameter only in the exceptional cases when it is unknown. Such rules can supply default values, or use some "weaker" information to approximate the value.

2.6.1.2 INITIALDATA and GOALS. The strategy of not tracing a parameter until some rule needs its value avoids needlessly tracing parameters whose values will never be used, but can mean that questions are asked in an order that appears random or unfamiliar to the client. To make the consultation more structured, each context type may have associated with it lists of parameters that the system builder expects will *always* be needed, and hence might as well be traced immediately. These lists are the **INITIALDATA** parameters (of the **ASKFIRST** variety) and **GOALS** parameters (whose tracing requires invoking rules). Whenever EMYCIN creates a new context during a consultation, it asks the client for each of the **INITIALDATA** parameters, and then traces the **GOALS** parameters. In fact, it is tracing the **GOALS** of the root of the context tree that initiates the consultation.

2.6.1.3 Tabular entry. It often happens that a knowledge base contains several related parameters that logically ought to be asked together. For example, in MYCIN the results of certain lab tests are expressed as several parameters, and it is certainly most convenient for the physician user to enter all the results at once if she has to look up any one of the results in the patient's chart anyway. However, if the parameters are asked only when each individually is required by a rule, not only are several questions asked, but they may not even be asked consecutively.

EMYCIN allows the system architect to specify that certain parameters are to be collected in "tabular" fashion. Whenever any of the parameters in a table is to be asked, the entire table is asked at once. For example, Figure 2-6 shows how MYCIN acquires the results of a battery of CSF tests. The **INITIALDATA** for several contexts of the same type may also be acquired compactly in a multiline table. Using the table has two desirable effects: (1) the questions are better ordered, and hence the consultation dialogue appears more coherent, and (2) it appears to the client that fewer questions are being asked, since several individual questions are being asked in one table. This latter effect is especially important in systems where reducing the number of questions is a significant consideration.

```
Please enter CSF findings in the following table:

        CSF        Percent   Protein   CSF        Peripheral
        WBC        PMN                 Glucose    Glucose
16) **  100        99        280       5          20
```

Figure 2-6. Five questions from a MYCIN consultation posed in "tabular" form.

A possible disadvantage of tabular input, of course, is that more information may be gathered than is actually needed for a particular consultation. At the time the question is asked, the system knows only that *one* of the parameters in the table is explicitly needed by a rule, leaving the possibility that one or more of the other parameters in the table will never be used. In some cases the system designer knows from the structure of the rule base that all of the information will eventually be used, but in general the designer must choose tables carefully, weighing the benefit of having the client conveniently enter several related pieces of information at once against the possible cost of gathering too much data.

2.6.1.4 Antecedent rules. The rules described so far are *consequent rules*, i.e., they are triggered by the need to find out information in their consequents (actions). In addition, EMYCIN permits a limited use of *antecedent rules*, which are triggered when the information in their antecedents (premises) becomes known. They have exactly the same form as consequent rules; they differ only in the conditions of their use. Whenever the system finishes tracing a parameter (or makes a definite conclusion, or receives new, definite data from the user), it retrieves the list of antecedent rules that test that parameter in their premises. It then applies each of these rules whose premise is now entirely known (i.e., no parameters remain to be traced).

Antecedent rules can be "chained forward," but only in a fairly restricted sense. The conclusion made by one antecedent rule can only trigger another rule if the conclusion is definite (thereby making the concluded parameter "traced" and causing the invocation of antecedent rules described above).[9] Conclusions made with less than certainty therefore have no effect on the control flow. This fundamental asymmetry also means that antecedent rules making less than definite conclusions have little use in any case—if the system ever needs to know the value of the parameter concluded in such a rule, it will have to go through the normal tracing mechanism anyway, and the antecedent rule might just as well have been a consequent rule.[10]

Furthermore, even in a system that does not use CF's, where all conclusions are definite, there is limited use for antecedent rules. Since they are simply demons waiting for their premises to become true, they never cause questions to be asked. If all the rules in the knowledge base were antecedent rules, the system would have to know ahead of time all the data that the problem would require for *any* case and would thus lose the benefits of questions tailored to the particular case.

Thus, the principal use for antecedent rules is to make definitional conclusions that one would not want to make via the normal backward-chained deductive mechanism. Concluding in an antecedent rule the value of a parameter **P** with certainty will prevent the asking or inferring of **P** later on, should it be needed for any reason. Ordinarily, a consequent rule could be used to make such a definitional inference, but there are two cases where this may not be true:

(a) **P** is an **ASKFIRST** parameter. In this case, the parameter would be asked before any consequent rules are tried.[11]

(b) Backward chaining is undesirable; i.e., the system should not actually trace the parameter(s) in the premise of the rule if they were not already known (it would be easier to ask **P** directly), but if it happened to have found them out for some other reason, then the information about **P** should be asserted, since asking a question about it or going to the effort of deducing it would be redundant.

A typical antecedent rule is shown in Figure 2-7. Ordinarily, the parameter *the patient has had a genito-urinary manipulative procedure* would be asked of the physician user directly; however, if the user has already told the system of a urine culture obtained by one of several methods of collection, this question would be redundant. The antecedent rule is triggered when the method of collection of the urine culture is found out, thereby in effect "answering" this subsequent question.

Rule091

```
If:   1) The site of the culture is urine, and
      2) The method of collection of the culture is one of:
         foley-cath-aspiration, foley-bag-drainage, straight-
         catheterization, ureteral

Then: It is definite (1.0) that the patient has had a genito-
      urinary manipulative procedure
```

Figure 2-7. An antecedent rule from MYCIN.

A special case of (a) permits the use of "conditional" **INITIALDATA**—
the system designer may specify a list of all the parameters that might
need to be asked for a context type, and have antecedent rules "prune"
the list. The pruning is accomplished by having antecedent rules use the
client's responses to early questions to answer the later questions in the
list, or to decide that some of them are now irrelevant. For example, in
MYCIN the **INITIALDATA** for an organism context includes the identity
of the organism, its gramstain, and its morphology. If the identity is unknown, the system asks the gramstain and morphology in the usual fashion; if the user knows the identity, however, the antecedent rule shown
in Figure 2-8 infers the gramstain and morphology directly from internal
tables of the known organisms, and those questions are never asked.

Rule155

    If: The laboratory-reported identity of the organism is known
          with certainty

    Then: It is definite (1.0) that these properties - gram, morph,
           air, genus - should be transferred from the
           laboratory-reported identity of the organism to this
           organism

Figure 2-8. A question-pruning antecedent rule.

Even non-**ASKFIRST** parameters can benefit from antecedent rules. Even
though a rule could be stated as a consequent rule and thereby be invoked
(along with perhaps many other rules) when it came time to trace the
parameter, a definitional antecedent rule can obviate the need to trace the
parameter at all. A similar, more general function is performed by Unitypath (Section 2.6.2.2), albeit less efficiently.[12]

2.6.1.5 Self-referencing rules.   In a pure backward-chained system, a
rule would not be permitted to reference in its premise the parameter that
appears in its action, as this would lead to a reasoning loop: in order to
evaluate the premise of the rule, the system would need to trace the very
parameter whose tracing invoked the rule in the first place. However,
EMYCIN does permit such "self-referencing rules"; typically they are
used to refine an existing conclusion, or to supply defaults when regular
rules have failed to make a conclusion. For example, the rule shown in
Figure 2-9 is one of a handful of "default" rules in CLOT—they say if,
after tracing, you have found no reason to believe a certain condition
exists, then assume it does not.

```
If:   It is not known whether there are factors that
      interfere with the patient's normal bleeding
Then: It is definite (1.0) that there are not factors that
      interfere with the patient's normal bleeding
```

Figure 2-9. Self-referencing rule supplying a default.

In order that self-referencing rules not cause looping or violate the assumption that the order within a set of rules for one parameter is arbitrary, the rule interpreter treats them as a separate rule set. It first applies the set of non-self-referencing rules in the usual fashion. It then applies the self-referencing rules, locally evaluating all references to the common parameter in terms of its (constant) value before any of the self-referencing rules was tried. Thus any conclusions made by the latter rule set are not "visible" until the entire set has been tried. The order of application within each of the two sets of rules is still arbitrary.

2.6.1.6 Metarules. *Metarules*, as defined by Davis [Davis 76], are available in EMYCIN as a more general means of affecting the control structure. Metarules are rules that operate on other rules; specifically, metarules are applied to the list of rules about to be invoked to deduce a parameter, and may reorder and/or prune that list. Reordering the list of rules may serve to provide better focus to the consultation dialogue—the metarules may stipulate that topics (parameters in the premises of the rules) be discussed in a particular order. Pruning the list is obviously useful when the list is large.

2.6.2 Focusing the Deductive Mechanism

The basic rule interpreter algorithm described thus far will, in most cases, trace parameters and ask questions only when needed. However, there are a couple of situations that arise that can result in tracing a parameter that in hindsight need not have been traced at all. By anticipating these situations, some improvement is possible in the simple algorithm.

2.6.2.1 Preview. The first improvement makes use of the fact that a conjunction is false if any of its component conjuncts is false. Ordinarily, the rule interpreter evaluates the clauses in a rule's premise in the order in which they appear, and stops in failure as soon as any clause is found to be false. However, if the false clause is not the first clause in the premise, some needless computation may have been performed in evaluating the clauses that appeared before the false clause. From this observation arises the *Preview* mechanism: when a rule is to be applied, the interpreter checks first to see if some clause in the premise is already known to be false on the basis of the parameters already traced; if so, the rule is not tried at all.

Preview does not save effort by eliminating rules per se, but it may avoid the tracing of a parameter in one of the clauses that the rule interpreter would otherwise have evaluated (i.e., one of the clauses earlier in the rule than the one found to be false). If that parameter is not required by any other rule, the system thereby saves the effort of inferring the parameter and/or asking what turns out to be an irrelevant question. If the process of inferring the parameter would itself cause the tracing of other parameters, the savings can be even more substantial. The effect can be thought of as pruning away some subgoal tree that has been discovered to be irrelevant.

2.6.2.2   *Unitypath.*

The second observation is that, according to the model of confirmation used in EMYCIN [Shortliffe 75], when the value of a parameter is concluded with certainty, no further rules to conclude that parameter need be tried—the definite value excludes all others. Thus it is best to try for the definite conclusion first. Before the interpreter traces a parameter, it examines the rules that conclude about the parameter and checks to see if there exists a rule whose premise is known with certainty and whose conclusion is definite. If so, the interpreter applies that rule immediately. The selected rule is termed a *Unitypath* to finding the value of the parameter.[13] The Unitypath procedure is followed for all parameters. When it succeeds for an **ASKFIRST** parameter, it saves asking the client a question; when it succeeds for ordinary parameters, it may have saved needlessly tracing some other parameters, viz., those which appear only in the rules that Unitypath prunes away (the same optimization obtained from Preview, except that Preview prunes away clauses from one rule, while Unitypath can in one stroke prune away many rules). It also has the effect of making "common sense" or definitional conclusions (those with CF = 1) happen immediately.

A further optimization along these lines, but one not currently performed by EMYCIN, might be to reorder the rules about to be applied so that rules with definite conclusions are tried first. It is not the same as the Unitypath procedure, since it simply means trying first the rules that *might* halt the tracing procedure soon, rather than applying the rule that is *known* to give the correct answer immediately. The difference is clearest in the case where all the rules in the set have definite conclusions—while simply reordering the rules would be a no-op (the rules are already trivially in order), Unitypath could still accomplish something (prune away rules and hence possibly subgoal trees).

Unitypath could be thought of as a global metarule that reads, "If there is a rule whose premise is already known with certainty, and whose conclusion has CF = 1, then apply *only* that rule."[14] The reordering suggested in the previous paragraph would be the simpler metarule, "If there are rules whose conclusion have CF = 1, then apply them before the other rules."

2.6.3   *More Details of the Rule Language*

This section is intended to give the reader a better idea of what sorts of statements can be expressed in rules. The conditions in the premises of rules are tested by *predicate* functions, either selected from the basic set provided by EMYCIN or programmed specially for particular applications. The predicates operate on fact triples, the specific nature of which is dependent on the contexts and parameters of the domain.

2.6.3.1   *Types of parameters.*   The parameters described thus far are termed "single-valued" parameters—their possible values are mutually exclusive, and hence such parameters can take on only one value with certainty, even though there may be several competing hypotheses. For example, *the identity of the organism* is such a parameter; while there may at any time be several hypotheses as to the identity, there is in fact only one "correct" value.

A special case of single-valued parameters that is commonly used is the "yes/no" parameter—it takes on the "values" **Yes** and **No** (or **True** and **False**). However, since these values are complementary and exhaustive, all the information is effectively tied to the CF: the CF can range from −1 (definitely false) to 1 (definitely true). The "value" **No** is simply **Yes** with negative certainty.

Another kind of parameter is possible: the *multivalued* parameter. It can assume several values at once; the values are not mutually exclusive. Conceptually, the value is a set. For example, consider the parameter *the drugs to which the patient is allergic*. It is certainly possible for a patient to be allergic to more than one drug at once; the value of this parameter might be "penicillin, ampicillin, not tetracycline," each individual value asserted with CF = 1.

Thus, if a multivalued parameter is being traced, the act of making a conclusion with certainty no longer terminates the tracing, as it does with single-valued parameters, since the one value does not exclude others. For the same reason, Unitypath is not applicable to multivalued parameters. Henceforth, any reference to early termination of tracing due to a definite conclusion shall be understood to apply only to single-valued parameters.

Since each individual value may be independently present or absent, a multivalued parameter may be thought of as shorthand for a set of single-valued, yes/no parameters, one for each possible value; e.g., "allergy = penicillin," "allergy = ampicillin," etc. However, the parameter is still traced as a single entity, not once for each value.

A multivalued parameter may also be defined to take on contexts as values; this feature can be used to create dynamic links between parts of the context tree (see Section 2.6.3.3 below).

2.6.3.2 *Predicates.* Predicates are the functions that test conditions in the premises of rules. They may be strictly true or false, or may assign a CF to the outcome of the test. The predicates supplied with EMYCIN fall roughly into the following classes:[15]

(1) predicates that test whether a parameter is or is not a specified value, with varying certainty ranges:

> *The site of the culture is blood.*
> *The patient might be febrile.*
> *The identity of the organism is definitely not E.Coli.*

(2) predicates that test with what certainty a parameter is known, independent of value:

> *The defective coagulation pathway of the patient is known.*
> *It is not known whether the organism is a contaminant.*
> *The identity of the organism is known with certainty.*

(3) numeric predicates for comparing ranges of numerical data:[16]

> *The age of the patient is greater than 6.*
> *The number of cultures is less than 3.*
> *The number of days since the culture was taken is between 2 and 5.*

(4) "mapping" functions (see Section 2.6.3.3 for further details), existential and selective:

> *There exists a positive culture such that ⟨predicate⟩.*
> *For all negative cultures it is true that ⟨predicate⟩.*
> *Find all substructures such that ⟨predicate⟩.*

(5) miscellaneous predicates:[17]

Disjunction:	*The genus of the organism is not known or*
	the genus of the organism is Streptococcus.
Control flow:	*The genus of the organism has been traced.*

We have found that new domains often need a small set of new predicates tailored to the domain. For example, the PUFF system includes predicates for comparing disease severities expressed symbolically as tokens such as "**MILD**," "**MODERATE**," and "**SEVERE**" (which could be thought of as generalizations of the numeric predicates in (3) above).[18]

2.6.3.3 Talking about the context tree.   Ordinarily, rules need not be explicitly concerned with the form of the context tree. When a rule is applied to a particular node in the tree (because the system is trying to find out the value of some parameter of the context), each reference to a parameter in the rule is "bound" to the obvious context—parameters of the current context are associated directly with it, while parameters of any context type higher in the tree are associated with the corresponding context that is found by climbing up the tree from the current node. For example, in the tree of Figure 2-2, if a rule applied to Organism-3 mentions *the site of the culture*, the system will associate *the culture* with Culture-2.

If a rule is applied to some context and uses information about contexts *lower* in the tree, however, an implicit iteration occurs: the rule is applied to each of the lower contexts in turn. If the lower contexts have not yet been instantiated, they are at this time (thus, contexts are instantiated because rules need them,[19] just as parameters are traced when rules need them). In fact, since the goals of the consultation usually consist of finding out something about the root of the tree, the only way that lower contexts get involved at all is when rules to conclude about the root use information about lower context types.

That works well for contexts that are in a direct ancestor/descendent relationship, but sometimes one wants to apply a rule to "disjoint" parts of the tree, or express a computation other than simply "apply this rule to all cases." For such purposes, EMYCIN supplies a set of mapping functions. These functions map over some set of contexts, e.g., all instances of a particular context type (all positive cultures), or the value of some context-valued parameter (all cultures thought to be relevant to the infection). The function tests each context for some condition (the condition takes the same form as that of a rule premise), and may select one or all contexts satisfying the condition. Selecting just one constitutes the existential predicate "there exists a *context* such that *condition*"; selecting all contexts satisfying the condition permits the rule to make conclusions about, or use information about, a whole set of contexts at once.

A special case of the latter, and one used most commonly, corresponds to applying a rule to the current node paired with all possible choices from some other part of the tree. Applying to **Context-A** a rule of the form:

Premise: Select all contexts in **list** that satisfy **condition**.

Action: Conclude for each selected **Context-B***i* something about
parameter of **Context-A**.

is effectively the same as applying the rule:

Premise: **Condition** of **Context-B***i* is true.

Action: Conclude something about **parameter** of **Context-A**.

to **Context-A** once for each **Context-B***i* in **list**, and thus is similar to the implicit mapping that occurs when the **Context-B***i*'s are direct descendents of **Context-A**. The values being concluded are usually a function of the selected context, however, rather than constants. For example, MYCIN employs several mapping rules to infer the identity of an organism from the identity of other organisms in the case; one such rule is shown in Figure 2-10. A major shortcoming of mapping rules in EMYCIN is that the similarity between them and rules that involve an implicit iteration is totally obscured by the need to explicitly describe the iteration set and context bindings (this is discussed further in Section 6.1.2).

<u>Rule182</u>

```
If:    1) The site of the culture is csf, and
       2) You have examined the organisms isolated from positive
          cultures obtained from the patient, selecting every
          organism for which
          A: The site of this culture is one of: those sites that
             are normally sterile,
          B: The site of this culture is not one of: middle-ear
             blood csf,
          C: The identity of this organism is known with certainty,
          D: The organism under consideration and this organism have
             the same value for the stain of the organism,
          E: The organism under consideration and this organism have
             the same value for the morphology of the organism, and
          F: There is significant disease associated with this
             occurrence of this organism
Then:  There is weakly suggestive evidence (.3) that the
          information that you have gathered about the identity of
          each of the organisms that you selected is also relevant
          to this organism
```

Figure 2-10. A mapping rule from MYCIN that examines several organisms at once.

2.6.4 The Certainty Factor Mechanism

For completeness, it should be pointed out that the certainty factor model described at length in [Shortliffe 75], and used in the original MYCIN system, is slightly different from the one currently in use in EMYCIN.[20] The difference concerns the manner in which evidence from several sources (multiple rules) for a single hypothesis (fact triple) is combined into one certainty measure. The Shortliffe paper uses the concepts *measure of belief in a hypothesis h, based on evidence e*($MB[h,e]$) and *measure of disbelief* (MD) similarly; MB and MD are numbers in the range [0,1]. The combined certainty is then defined as

$$CF = MB - MD,$$

which is in the range [-1,1]. For any single rule, only one of MB and MD is nonzero (for positive rules, it is MB; for negative rules, it is MD, actually written as CF = -MD). The MB's and MD's are accumulated independently and combined in the end to produce the final CF. The formula to accumulate MB's is

$$MB[h,e_1\&e_2] = MB[h,e_1] + MB[h,e_2](1-MB[h,e_1]),$$

and similarly for MD's.

The scheme currently used by EMYCIN, on the other hand, defines CF as[21]

$$CF = \frac{MB - MD}{1 - \min\{MB,MD\}},$$

which is obviously the same when MB or MD is zero, but has the property that CF's of the same or opposite sign can be combined directly, by the following commutative formula:

$$cfcombine\,(x,y) = \begin{cases} x + y\,(1-x), & \text{if } x \text{ and } y \text{ are positive;} \\[2mm] \dfrac{x + y}{1 - \min\{|x|, |y|\}}, & \text{if } xy < 0; \\[2mm] -cfcombine\,(-x,-y), & \text{if } x \text{ and } y \text{ are negative.} \end{cases}$$

[Additionally, combining 1 and −1 (which should never happen, of course) is defined to yield 1, to avoid the singularity at that point.]

This scheme is identical to the old one for combining CF's of like sign, but is more gentle when combining CF's of opposite sign. The previous scheme had the problem of compressing too much information into the region near 1. As a result, ten conclusions of CF = .9 could get substantially knocked down by a single conclusion of CF = −.8.

Also, since the new formula is commutative, it is no longer necessary to accumulate separate MB's and MD's; a single CF is accumulated, reflecting at once both positive and negative evidence.

2.7   Review of Applications

It might be useful at this point to examine the structure of some of the applications in terms of the architectural features described above, to get a better idea of what use has been made of which features. Figure 2-11 describes the five knowledge bases of Section 1.2 by the size of their rule and parameter sets and the distribution of rules.

As is evident from Rows 4 and 5, only about half of the parameters in these domains are concluded by rules; the remainder are "input data" prompted for by the program. Rows 7 and 8 indicate, for just the parameters that are concluded in rules or used by rules, respectively, the number of rules that conclude or use the parameter. The mean in these rows does not sufficiently tell the full story, as there is high variance in the distribution of rules to parameter. For example, there is one parameter in MYCIN that is concluded by ninety-three rules, yet half of the parameters are concluded by only one or two rules.[22] Similarly, there is one parameter[23] that is used in one-third of the rules, but most parameters are used in only a few. It is interesting to note that, independent of the size of the knowledge base, the median number of rules concluded or used is small and nearly constant; and even the maximum number is fairly consistent across systems (except for Row 7 of PUFF) when expressed as a percentage of the total number of rules.

Knowledge base:	MYCIN	HEADMED	SACON	PUFF	CLOT
1. total number of rules	451	232	165	63	54
2. number of antecedent rules	39	4	2	7	0
3. number of context types	13	12	4	1	1
4. total number of parameters	191	63	52	48	55
5. number of parameters concluded by rules	104	26	25	25	20
6. number of (5) that can also be asked	36	4	6	0	2
7. mean number of rules per parameter concluded	5	9	9	4	3
median	2	3	4	2	2
maximum	93	58	45	32	13
as % of (1)	20%	25%	27%	50%	24%
standard deviation	13	16	13	6	3
8. mean number of rules per parameter used	8	9	17	4	4
median	3	4	9	2	3
maximum	151	57	50	21	22
as % of (1)	33%	24%	30%	33%	40%
standard deviation	19	12	17	4	4

Figure 2-11. Statistics for some EMYCIN knowledge bases.

The "mean number of rules per parameter concluded" (in Row 7) differs from the quotient of Row 1 by Row 5 in most cases because it is possible for a rule to conclude about more than one parameter; e.g., in the PUFF knowledge base, fully half of the rules conclude about two or more parameters.

2.7.1   Use of Antecedent Rules

Close to 10% of the rules in MYCIN and PUFF are antecedent rules, but the other knowledge bases made scant use of them. Consistent with the constraints outlined above (Section 2.6.1.4), all of the antecedent rules in these systems make "definitional" conclusions, print messages, or mark certain parameters "irrelevant"; none make judgmental conclusions.

2.7.2 Asking vs. Inferring

Although the rule interpreter provides for asking the client a question when rules fail (or in the case of ASKFIRST parameters, before rules are tried), in most of the systems there is a fairly clear distinction between "input" parameters, whose values are requested from the client rather than being inferred by rules, and "output" parameters, concluded by rules but never asked. Row 6 indicates the size of the overlap for each system. The dichotomy is sharpest in PUFF, where *no* parameter is both asked and concluded. Furthermore, of the 25 parameters in that system concluded by rules, 20 are concluded solely by consequent rules, the remaining five solely by antecedent rules.

In the other systems, at least some of the parameters concluded by rules are also askable. In SACON and CLOT, none of them is ASKFIRST, meaning that they will only be asked when the rules fail. In HEADMED, one of the four parameters in the overlap is ASKFIRST; its rule is thus used to conclude a default value if the client fails to respond.

The greatest diversity occurs in MYCIN, where of the 104 parameters whose values can be concluded by rules, 36 are askable, and 6 of those are ASKFIRST parameters (two use rules to conclude "default" values, another three can be deduced via alternative methods, and the remaining parameter has only definitional rules (usually found by Unitypath) to avoid asking the question in the first place[24]).

2.7.3 Use of Certainty Factors

SACON does not use CF's at all; all rules make definite conclusions. The other systems use CF's to varying degrees; CF's make no sense associated with numeric parameters,[25] and nearly all "input" parameters are known with certainty.[26] CF's were designed in MYCIN to be merely an approximate measure of certainty, and indeed a study of the use of CF's in MYCIN [Clancey 79b] has demonstrated the highly approximate nature of CF's. Small perturbations in the CF's of the rule conclusions made little difference in the final outcome; the system behaved approximately consistent with a certainty model in which the CF's were replaced by four or five certainty ranges (corresponding to the intervals delimited by 0, .2, .4, .6, .8, 1.0).

2.7.4 Use of Metarules

None of the systems currently uses metarules. One of the primary stated motivations for developing metarules was to handle cases of large rule sets in which exhaustive invocation of rules is too ill-focused to be effective or efficient; however, none of the applications has yet had this problem to any significant degree.

2.7.5   *Other Observations*

The value of a parameter is not always a number or a word from a predefined set; rules may also conclude arbitrary text strings, to be printed out as results, recommendations, etc. EMYCIN supplies a simple function to neatly display such results. The PUFF rule shown in Figure 2-12 illustrates this use of text strings.

```
If:    1) The degree of obstructive airways disease of the patient
          is greater than or equal to mild,
       2) The degree of diffusion defect of the patient is
          greater than or equal to mild, and
       3) The total lung capacity measured by the body box (TLCB)
          is greater than 110 percent of predicted,

Then:  1) There is strongly suggestive evidence (.9) that the subtype
          of obstructive airways disease is emphysema, and
       2) The following is one of the conclusion statements about
          this interpretation: "The low diffusing capacity, in
          combination with obstruction and a high total lung capacity
          would be consistent with a diagnosis of emphysema."
```

Figure 2-12. A sample rule from PUFF that uses an arbitrary text string, rather than a value from a predefined set, as one of its conclusions.

As might be expected, MYCIN makes use of almost all of EMYCIN's features. It makes much more use of mapping rules than the other knowledge bases. MYCIN has many domain-specific predicates and specialized code, the principal instance being for the process of therapy selection, which proved too difficult to express in rules. MYCIN instead has a therapy module that uses a generate and test algorithm [Clancey 77]; rules are still used for the "test" part. The QA module has considerable domain-specific additions, principally to explain the therapy selection process. Its dictionary comprises 1800 terms.

3

An Example

To show the interaction between EMYCIN and the system designer, this chapter presents an extended example of how one might use EMYCIN to create an initial knowledge base in a new domain. What follows are excerpts from an actual typescript of a session with EMYCIN; the domain is the diagnosis of human coagulative disorders.[1] This session is merely the first of a series of sessions in which the knowledge base is constructed and debugged, but provides an indication of the major activities involved in knowledge base construction. Chapter 4 explains the mechanisms behind this example.

Before coming to this session, the system designer has spent time, presumably with the domain expert (unless the designer is herself the expert), formulating the domain knowledge into rules and parameters, and has some sort of overall structure of the problem in mind. EMYCIN provides no direct assistance for this initial phase, but assumes that the designer has come prepared to enter a knowledge base whose gross structure is already known. What follows shows how the initial set of rules and parameters is entered and debugged using EMYCIN.

As always, user input appears in **BOLD ITALICS**, and annotations appear in *light italics*. User inputs generally occur after a prompt of a colon, question mark, or double asterisk. For those inputs for which the user (system designer) types only part of the input, with the rest completed by the system, only the user's part is in bold italics.[2] In addition, for those user inputs consisting solely of a carriage return (blank line), the symbol ⏎ is employed to distinguish this case from no input at all.

Do you wish to create a new knowledge base? *Yes*

> *When* EMYCIN *is first started, it goes through the following routine to define the context tree, i.e., the context types of the domain and the hierarchy that will determine how the dynamic context tree for a particular consultation will be organized. Once the context tree is defined,* EMYCIN *has a structure on which it can organize the rules and parameters of the domain.*

Enter a word or phrase to describe your domain, i.e. fill in the
    blank in "this program performs a ---- consultation". (e.g.
    infectious disease, structural analysis).
** *bleeding disorder*

Enter a one-word name for the root of your context tree, the
    central "object" with which the consultation is concerned
    (e.g. PATIENT, STRUCTURE).
** *PATIENT*

> *Start with the root of the tree. The name selected
> by the designer here will serve as a default
> translation in several places.*

Please enter a word or phrase as "translation" of PATIENT:
** patient -- Okay? Yes

> *The system prints its own suggestion after the "**" prompt, and the designer
> can accept it with one keystroke. If the suggestion is incorrect, the designer
> may refine it by editing it or reject it altogether and supply a new value.[3] In the
> present case, the designer accepts all suggestions, at least initially; one can
> always come back later to modify one of these choices. These translations will
> be used when the system talks about this type of context.*

And the plural form is:
** patients -- Okay? Yes

> *Irregular plurals do exist, of course.*

Give me a unique, 2-letter abbreviation for PATIENT:
** *PT*

Parameter group: PATIENT-PARMS -- Okay? Yes

> *Each context type has associated with it a list of
> parameters. This "question" serves to inform the
> designer of the name being assigned to that group,
> while allowing the designer to select another name
> if desired.*

PATIENT
PRINTID: PATIENT- -- Okay? Yes

> *This is the identifier that is used to create print
> names for contexts of this type, by appending digits;
> e.g., PATIENT-1.*

Enter a list of parameters which will always be asked of the user
    when a PATIENT is created:
PATIENT
INITIALDATA: *(NAME AGE SEX RACE REASON)*

> *Since this is the root node, these can be thought of
> as the "input" parameters of the program. They
> will constitute the first questions asked during every
> consultation.*

And now a list of parameters to infer whenever a PATIENT is
    created:
PATIENT
GOALS: *(FINALDEF CONSISTENT DX)*

> *And these are the output, or "result" parameters.*
> *After the* INITIALDATA *parameters are asked,*
> EMYCIN *will trace these parameters, which process*
> *will drive the rest of the consultation.*

Do you want the program to automatically display the values
    concluded for some or all of the GOALS? **Yes**
Which ones? (<cr> for all): *)*

> *The program will want to display the results of the consultation in some fashion,*
> *of course. The easiest way initially is simply to have* EMYCIN *print the values*
> *concluded for the* GOALS *in a default manner. Later, the designer might choose*
> *to write rules instead to display conclusions only under certain conditions, or to*
> *write a fancier conclusion printer.*

Now please define each of the parameters listed above. [Each is
    a member of PATIENT-PARMS].

> *The* GOALS *and* INITIALDATA *are both lists of parameters, which must be*
> *defined further by the designer.* EMYCIN *knows that the* INITIALDATA
> *parameters should have* PROMPT*'s (since they will be asked), and the*
> ASKFIRST *property;* GOALS *are concluded, rather than asked, so they have no*
> *prompts. These considerations affect which properties* EMYCIN *prompts for in*
> *the following.*

What kind of parm is NAME -- Yes/no, Singlevalued,
    Multivalued, or Ask-All? *Singlevalued*

> *This question further classifies the parameter*
> *according to the nature of the values it can take on.*
> *The answer to the question sets certain properties*
> *and affects which other properties need to be*
> *prompted for.*

NAME
EXPECT: *ANY*

> *The type of value (any) that the parameter can take*
> *on.*

NAME
TRANS: *(the name of *)*

> *How to translate uses of this parameter, e.g., in*
> *rules. The* * *in a* TRANS *or* PROMPT *is filled with*
> *the translation of the context associated with the*
> *parameter;* [4] *in this case, the patient.*

NAME
PROMPT: *(Name:)*

> *How to ask the client for the value during a*
> *consultation.*

```
What kind of parm is AGE -- Yes/no, Singlevalued,
    Multivalued, or Ask-All? Singlevalued
AGE
EXPECT: POSNUMB
```
The parameter takes on positive numbers for value.

```
AGE
UNITS: YEARS
```
Since it now knows that this is a numeric-valued parameter, EMYCIN asks for the units in which it is measured. This allows the client to answer, for example, "7 MONTHS" to the age question, and have the answer properly converted for use by the rest of the system.

```
AGE
TRANS: (the age of *)
AGE
PROMPT: (Age:)
```

```
What kind of parm is SEX -- Yes/no, Singlevalued,
    Multivalued, or Ask-All? Singlevalued
SEX
EXPECT: (MALE FEMALE)
```
An explicit list of expected values.

```
SEX
TRANS: (the sex of *)
SEX
PROMPT: (Sex:)
```

```
What kind of parm is RACE -- Yes/no, Singlevalued,
    Multivalued, or Ask-All? Singlevalued
RACE
EXPECT: (CAUCASIAN BLACK INDIAN ASIAN)
RACE
TRANS: (the race of *)
RACE
PROMPT: (Race:)
```

```
What kind of parm is REASON -- Yes/no, Singlevalued,
    Multivalued, or Ask-All? Ask-All
```

"Ask-All" parameters are multivalued parameters that are asked of the client in one question (the client responds with one or more values); normal multivalued parameters are asked one value at a time, in the yes/no format of "Is ⟨parameter⟩ = ⟨value⟩?"

```
REASON
EXPECT: (BLEEDING-HISTORY PRE-OP ANTI-COAG-THERAPY)
REASON
TRANS: (the reason for this consultation)
REASON
PROMPT: (Indicate your reason(s) for requesting this consultation:)
```

Now the GOALS will be defined. There is less information to enter here, since these parameters are never asked. The goals in CLOT are a final determination of the blood defect of the patient (FINALDEF), whether the clinical and laboratory estimates of this defect are consistent with each other (CONSISTENT), and a more specific diagnosis of enzymatic or platelet defect (DX).

```
What kind of parm is FINALDEF -- Yes/no,
    Singlevalued, Multivalued, or Ask-All? Multivalued
```
> *Recall that multivalued parameters are those whose values are not mutually exclusive: multiple values can be assumed at once.*
```
FINALDEF
LEGALVALS: (COAGULATION-DEFECT PLATELET-VASCULAR-DEFECT)
```
> *The LEGALVALS property for multivalued parameters is analogous to the EXPECT property.*
```
FINALDEF
TRANS: (the final blood disorders of *)
```

```
What kind of parm is CONSISTENT -- Yes/no,
    Singlevalued, Multivalued, or Ask-All? Yes/no
```
> *"Yes/no" parameters are single-valued parameters that take on the "values" yes and no (true and false).*
```
CONSISTENT
TRANS: (there is a consistent estimation of * 's blood disorder)
```
> *The translation of a yes/no parameter, rather than being a noun phrase, is stated as a predicate; to translate "⟨parameter⟩ = no", the system simply inserts the word not in an appropriate place.*

```
What kind of parm is DX -- Yes/no, Singlevalued,
    Multivalued, or Ask-All? Multivalued
DX
LEGALVALS: TEXT
```
> *This indicator means that DX takes on arbitrary text strings as value. Making statements of diagnostic conclusions is a common use for text strings in EMYCIN.*
```
DX
TRANS: (the blood coagulation diagnoses of *)
```

That takes care of all of the initial parameters.

```
[Okay, now back to PATIENT for one last property...]
PATIENT
SYN: (((NAME) (NAME))) -- Yes, No, or Edit? Yes
```

This property is a sort of TRANS *for context types, indicating how to translate the context instance itself. This one is a fairly simple form, saying simply to use the* NAME *parameter of the patient for a translation. More complex forms are possible, whereby one or more parameters of the context can be conditionally formed into a longer phrase, e.g., in* MYCIN *a culture context could be translated by way of its* SITE *parameter as "the blood culture".*

```
Creating rule group PATIENTRULES to apply to PATIENT contexts...
```

A rule group is automatically defined for each context type. It is also possible for the designer to define groups that apply to more than one type of context (see Section 4.1.4).

```
[finished with PATIENT]

   ...Autosave... <VANMELLE>CHANGES.;1
```

EMYCIN *has been keeping track of all the changes entered by the designer, and periodically saves them on a file to guard against machine crashes.*

```
Are there any descendents of PATIENT in the context tree? No
```

If this domain had a nontrivial context tree, the designer would continue describing the context types, entering the same sorts of information as shown above for the root.

At this point, having defined the skeletal structure of the domain (the context tree, input and output parameters), the designer can start entering rules and further parameters in earnest. The designer is now inside the top-level EMYCIN *executive, which switches among various routines in the knowledge base editor or chooses other operations that may be desired at some later point.*

```
Do you want to enter Rules, Parms, Go, etc (? for help) ? ?
```

Typing "?" invokes a help response, in this case listing explicitly the alternatives (all of these are one-character responses, chosen to be reasonably mnemonic).

```
one of:
Rule entry
Parameters
Contexts
Variables, random properties, etc.
Save changes so far on a file
Go -- run the consultation program
New consultation
Lisp -- drop into the Interlisp executive
Debug/review the results of the consultation
Explanation system (QA Module)
Quit -- exit EMYCIN
OK -- Return from this EMYCIN executive
```

Do you want to enter Rules, Parms, Go, etc (? for help) ? **Parameters**

> *Before entering any rules, the designer chooses to define a few more parameters that will be used in rules to conclude the specified goals. The parameter editor we have already seen in part above, where the INITIALDATA and GOALS were defined. This time, however, the designer has the initiative, specifying which parameters to define or modify at each point. This being the initial session, most of the time is spent defining new parameters, whereas in later sessions the parameter editor may be used more to modify (edit) existing parameters.*

Parameter name: **LABDEF**
Group for new parm LABDEF : **PATIENT-PARMS**

> *Each new parameter is assigned to a group, thereby determining which kinds of context it can belong to. Here* **P** *is sufficient to identify the* PATIENT-PARMS *group.*

What kind of parm is LABDEF -- Yes/no, Singlevalued,
    Multivalued, or Ask-All? **Multivalued**
LABDEF
LEGALVALS: **LIKE FINALDEF**

> EMYCIN *provides several commands to reduce the typing load, here one to copy a value from a parameter already defined.*

Copying LEGALVALS of FINALDEF:
        (COAGULATION-DEFECT PLATELET-VASCULAR-DEFECT)
LABDEF
TRANS: **(the blood defects of * (based on the coagulation screen
... test only))**

> *The "..." in this and subsequent interactions is a continuation-line prompt printed by the system to indicate that it is still waiting for the value started on the previous line to be terminated.*

LABDEF
PROMPT: **)**

> *The absence of a* PROMPT *indicates that this parameter is never asked. Unlike the* GOALS *parameters,* EMYCIN *cannot tell a priori that this is the case, so had to ask.*

Enter any more props now for LABDEF ? **No**

> EMYCIN *offers the designer an opportunity to enter optional properties, or to go back and fix any of those just entered.*

Parameter name: **CLINDEF**

> *More parameters are now entered in similar fashion...*

Group for new parm CLINDEF : **PATIENT-PARMS**
What kind of parm is CLINDEF -- Yes/no, Singlevalued,
    Multivalued, or Ask-All? **Multivalued**

```
CLINDEF
LEGALVALS: LIKE FINALDEF
Copying LEGALVALS of FINALDEF:
        (COAGULATION-DEFECT PLATELET-VASCULAR-DEFECT)
CLINDEF
TRANS: (the blood defects of * (based on clinical evidence only))
CLINDEF
PROMPT: )
Enter any more props now for CLINDEF ? No
```

```
Parameter name: DEFPATH
Group for new parm DEFPATH : PATIENT-PARMS
What kind of parm is DEFPATH -- Yes/no, Singlevalued,
    Multivalued, or Ask-All? Singlevalued
DEFPATH
EXPECT: (INTRINSIC EXTRINSIC COMMON MULTIPLE/FIBRIN)
DEFPATH
TRANS: (the defective coagulation pathway of *)
DEFPATH
PROMPT: )
Enter any more props now for DEFPATH ? No
```

```
Parameter name: SIGBLEED
Group for new parm SIGBLEED : PATIENT-PARMS
What kind of parm is SIGBLEED -- Yes/no,
    Singlevalued, Multivalued, or Ask-All? Yes/no
SIGBLEED
TRANS: (there is an episode of significant bleeding in *)
SIGBLEED
PROMPT: (Do you believe that the bleeding episode in * is
 ... significant?)
SIGBLEED
ASKFIRST: )
```

> *Since the designer has said that this parameter may be asked during a consultation, it becomes relevant whether to ask first before trying rules, or to ask only if rules fail. For this parameter, the ASKFIRST property is NIL (absent)—rules will be tried first.*

```
Enter any more props now for SIGBLEED ? No
```

```
Parameter name: BLDTYPE
Group for new parm BLDTYPE : PATIENT-PARMS
What kind of parm is BLDTYPE -- Yes/no, Singlevalued,
    Multivalued, or Ask-All? Ask-All
BLDTYPE
EXPECT: (TONSILLECTOMY ORAL-SURGERY EPISTAXIC PURPURA
 ... HEMARTHROSIS HEMOPTYSIS HEMATCHESIA HEMATEMESIS GU-BLEED)
```

```
BLDTYPE
TRANS: (the types of bleeding in *)
BLDTYPE
PROMPT: (What type of bleeding describes * 's most recent episode
   ... of bleeding?)
BLDTYPE
ASKFIRST: T
Enter any more props now for BLDTYPE ? No


Parameter name: )
```

A null parameter name terminates this routine.

```
Rules, Parms, Go, etc. ? Rules
```

The designer now enters rules, starting with rules to conclude the goals defined above. The first two rules say that the final conclusions regarding a blood defect (FINALDEF) are the accumulated conclusions using clinical evidence (CLINDEF) and laboratory evidence (LABDEF), when those two are consistent. The rules are stated in a stylized shorthand that uses the parameter names and values as operands (see Section 4.1.1).

```
Rule# or NEW: NEW
```

Alternatively, one can examine or modify an existing rule by supplying its number here.

```
RULE001
PREMISE: (CLINDEF IS KNOWN AND CONSISTENT)
RULE001
ACTION: (FINALDEF = CLINDEF)
```

EMYCIN *parses and checks the rule just entered.*

```
Translate, No further change, or prop name: TRANSLATE
```

The designer may go back to edit one of the properties just entered, set new properties (e.g., make this be an antecedent rule), or display the rule in several forms. Here the designer chooses to see the English translation of the rule.

```
RULE001
-------
   If:  1) The blood defects of the patient (based on clinical
           evidence only) are known, and
        2) There is a consistent estimation of the patient's blood
           disorder
   Then: It is definite (1.0) that the blood defects of the
           patient (based on clinical evidence only) is the
           final blood disorders of the patient
```

Since no CF *was explicitly given in the action, the default certainty of (1.0) was assumed.*

```
Translate, No further change, or prop name: PP
```

> *This command prettyprints the* LISP *form of the rule, showing into what internal form the rule was translated by the system.*

```
RULE001
-------
  PREMISE:  ($AND (KNOWN CNTXT CLINDEF)
                  (SAME CNTXT CONSISTENT))
  ACTION:   (TRANSDIFPARM CNTXT CLINDEF CNTXT FINALDEF 1000)
```

Translate, No further change, or prop name: *)*

> *No further action on this rule, so we move on to the next.*

```
Rule# or NEW: NEW
RULE002
PREMISE: (LABDEF IS KNOWN AND CONSISTENT)
RULE002
ACTION: (FINALDEF = LABDEF)
```

Translate, No further change, or prop name: *)*

```
Rule# or NEW: NEW
```

> *This will be the first of two rules for concluding the goal parameter* CONSISTENT *(that the clinical and laboratory conclusions are consistent with each other).*

```
RULE003
PREMISE: (CLINDEF = PLATELET-VASCULAR-DEFECT AND
    ... LABDEF = PLATELET-VASCUAR-DEFECT)
RULE003
ACTION: (CONSISTENT)
```

PLATELET-VASCUAR-DEFECT -> PLATELET-VASCULAR-DEFECT ? Yes

> *In the course of checking this rule,* EMYCIN *finds an incorrect value for the parameter* LABDEF. *The spelling corrector finds a likely correction by examining the set of legal values for that parameter.*

Translate, No further change, or prop name: *)*

```
Rule# or NEW: NEW
RULE004
PREMISE: (CLINDEF = COAGULATION-DEFECT AND
    ...      LABDEF = COAGULATION-DEFECT)
RULE004
ACTION: (CONSISTENT)
```

Translate, No further change, or prop name:)

Rule# or NEW: *NEW*

> *Now working backward from the main goal, the designer writes rules to conclude about one of the subgoals,* CLINDEF.

RULE005
PREMISE: *(SIGBLEED AND FAMILY)*
RULE005
ACTION: *(CLINDEF = COAGULATION-DEFECT (.3))*

Is FAMILY a new parameter ? *Yes*

> *In the course of parsing the rule,* EMYCIN *found* FAMILY *where it was expecting to find a parameter. It does not resemble any existing parameter, so* EMYCIN *asks if it is new, and now prompts the designer to define the new parameter.*

(in group PATIENT-PARMS)

> *Since there is only one type of context, this is the only group this parameter could be in, so the choice is automatic.*

What kind of parm is FAMILY -- Yes/no, Singlevalued,
    Multivalued, or Ask-All? *Yes/no*
FAMILY
TRANS: *(there is a history of a genetic bleeding disorder in*
    ... * 's family)
FAMILY
PROMPT: *T*

> *The value of* T *for the* PROMPT *indicates that the parameter is askable, but the designer is not specifying a particular way to ask it.[5]*

FAMILY
ASKFIRST: *T*

[back to RULE005 now]
Translate, No further change, or prop name: *TRANSLATE*

RULE005

   If: 1) There is an episode of significant bleeding in the
           patient, and
        2) There is a history of a genetic bleeding disorder in
           the patient's family
   Then: There is weakly suggestive evidence (.3) that
           coagulation-defect is one of the blood defects of the
           patient (based on clinical evidence only)

Translate, No further change, or prop name:)

Rule# or NEW: *NEW*
RULE006
PREMISE: *(SIGBLED AND ONSET = DELAYED)*
RULE006
ACTION: *LIKE 5*

Similar to the shorthand used to enter the LEGALVALS of LABDEF above. Here "5" stands for "RULE005".

Copying ACTION of RULE005:
        (CONCLUDE CNTXT CLINDEF COAGULATION-DEFECT TALLY 300)

SIGBLED -> SIGBLEED ? *Yes*

Spelling correction, this time using the list of all parameter names, since a parameter is expected here.

Is ONSET a new parameter ? *Yes*

(in group PATIENT-PARMS)

What kind of parm is ONSET -- Yes/no, Singlevalued,
    Multivalued, or Ask-All? *Singlevalued*
ONSET
EXPECT: *(IMMEDIATE DELAYED)*
ONSET
TRANS: *(the onset of * 's bleeding)*
ONSET
PROMPT: *(Was the onset of bleeding immediate or delayed?)*
ONSET
ASKFIRST: *T*

[back to RULE006 now]
Translate, No further change, or prop name: *)*

Rule# or NEW: *NEW*
RULE007
PREMISE: *(SIGBLEED, BLDTYPE = HEMARTHROSIS AND*
    ... BLDTYPE ~= PETECHIAE)
RULE007
ACTION: *(CLINDEF = COAGULATION-DEFECT .3)*

Is PETECHIAE a new value for BLDTYPE ? *Yes*

This was not one of the expected values the designer supplied when defining BLDTYPE. EMYCIN now updates the EXPECT property of BLDTYPE in the background. Unlike with new parameters, no further information is needed at this point.

    ...Autosave... <VANMELLE>CHANGES.;2

Translate, No further change, or prop name:)

Rule# or NEW: *NEW*
RULE008
PREMISE: *(SIGBLEED, BLDTYPE ~= HEMARTHROSIS AND*
 ... BLDTYPE = PETECHIAE)
RULE008
ACTION: *(CLINDEF = PLATELET-VASCULAR-DEFECT .3)*
Translate, No further change, or prop name:)

Rule# or NEW:)

> *Null response exits the rule editor and brings us back to the top level again.*

Rules, Parms, Go, etc. ? **Parameters**

> *Before entering rules to conclude* LABDEF, *the designer goes back to the parameter editor to define the parameters that make up the battery of coagulation screen tests.*

Parameter name: *PT*
Group for new parm PT : PATIENT-PARMS
What kind of parm is PT -- Yes/no, Singlevalued,
 Multivalued, or Ask-All? *Singlevalued*
PT
EXPECT: *(LOW NORMAL HIGH)*
PT
TRANS: *(the prothrombin time)*
PT
PROMPT:)
Enter any more props now for PT ? *No*

Parameter name: *PTT*
PTT=PT ? *No*

> *Since the designer could be modifying an existing parameter, the parameter editor first checks that this is not just a misspelling. This attempted correction is the result of choosing names that look too much alike.*

Group for new parm PTT : PATIENT-PARMS
What kind of parm is PTT -- Yes/no, Singlevalued,
 Multivalued, or Ask-All? *Singlevalued*
PTT
EXPECT: *LIKE PT*
Copying EXPECT of PT: (LOW NORMAL HIGH)

```
PTT
TRANS: (the activated partial thromboplastin time)
PTT
PROMPT: )
Enter any more props now for PTT ? No
```

. . .

> *In similar fashion the expert now defines* TT *(the thrombin time),* BT *(the bleeding time), and* PC *(the platelet count). Like* PT *and* PTT *just defined, these parameters are all expressed as ranges (e.g., low, normal, high), which will be inferred from the raw laboratory data defined next.*

```
Parameter name: NPT
```

> *This parameter will be the numeric input parameter from which* PT *is inferred.*

```
Group for new parm NPT : PATIENT-PARMS
What kind of parm is NPT -- Yes/no, Singlevalued,
    Multivalued, or Ask-All? Singlevalued
NPT
EXPECT: POSNUMB
NPT
UNITS: SECONDS
```

> *Again, numeric-valued parameters may have associated units.*

```
Should I add SECONDS to UNITNAMES ? Yes
```

> *...and the property checker knows that all units are assumed to be on this internal list.*

```
NPT
TRANS: (the numeric value of the prothrombin time)
NPT
PROMPT: (PT:)
```

> *The standard lab abbreviation is used as a prompt here.*

```
NPT
ASKFIRST: T
Enter any more props now for NPT ? No
```

. . .

> *In similar fashion, the designer now defines numeric parameters* NPTT, NTT, NBT *and* NPC *to correspond to the other 4 symbolic parameters (*PTT, TT, BT, PC).

. . .

```
Parameter name: FSF
```
This is one last laboratory test, not expressed numerically.
```
Group for new parm FSF : PATIENT-PARMS
What kind of parm is FSF -- Yes/no, Singlevalued,
    Multivalued, or Ask-All? Singlevalued
FSF
EXPECT: (NORMAL ABNORMAL)
FSF
TRANS: (the urea solubility)
FSF
PROMPT: (FSF:)
FSF
ASKFIRST: T
Enter any more props now for FSF ? No

Parameter name: )


Rules, Parms, Go, etc. ? Rules
```
The designer now defines rules to infer the symbolic parameters from the numeric laboratory measurements.
```
Rule# or NEW: NEW
RULE009
PREMISE: (NPT IS KNOWN)
RULE009
ACTION: (PT = TABLE)
```
Here TABLE is a pseudo-value that invokes a table-building routine. In what follows, the designer constructs a decision table on one condition (NPT) to infer the value of PT.
```
Creating a table to conclude PT
Numeric condition/parm to branch on: NPT
Possible values of PT to conclude (<cr> for all):
** )
```
For this rule the designer wants to conclude about all possible values. In more specialized applications the table could discuss just a subset of the legal values.
```
Enter a cf in each value column, or * to omit; end with blank line
```
*The designer specifies in each line a range for the condition, and which value(s) this implies for PT, in terms of a CF for the value in the header (1 = definitely yes, 0 or * = omitted, −1 = definitely no). Typing a tab advances to the next column. Where applicable, the system defaults the lower limit of the range to the upper limit of the preceding one (this is the most common case; designer can backspace over it and change it if desired). While the following table is comparatively trivial, concluding exactly one value for each range of the condition, some knowledge bases have more complex tables.*

```
If NPT
   is between:       then conclude value(s):
   low   high       LOW      NORMAL      HIGH
**  *    12.3        1
** 12.3  13.5        *         1
** 13.5  *           *         *          1
** )
```

Translate, No further change, or prop name: *TRANSLATE*

Here is what the rule looks like, as translated by EMYCIN *into somewhat stilted English:*

RULE009

```
   If:  The numeric value of the prothrombin time is known
   Then:  The prothrombin time is as follows:
          If the numeric value of the prothrombin time is:
          a) less than 12.3 seconds then: low (1.0);
          b) between 12.3 seconds and 13.5 seconds then: normal
             (1.0);
          c) greater or equal to 13.5 seconds then: high (1.0);
```

Translate, No further change, or prop name: *PP*

...which is accomplished by the function CONCLUDET, *a simple decision table interpreter.*

RULE009

```
   PREMISE:  ($AND (KNOWN CNTXT NPT))
   ACTION:   (CONCLUDET CNTXT (VAL1 CNTXT NPT)
                '((LT 12.3 1000)
                  (BT 12.3 13.5 0 1000)
                  (GE 13.5 0 0 1000))
                TALLY PT '(LOW NORMAL HIGH))
```

Translate, No further change, or prop name:)

· · ·

In similar fashion, the designer writes rules to infer PTT *from* NPTT, TT *from* NTT, PC *from* NPC, *and* BT *from* NBT.

· · ·

Finally ready now to write rules to conclude the other main subgoal, LABDEF.

```
Rule# or NEW: NEW
RULE014
PREMISE: (DEFPATH IS KNOWN)
RULE014
ACTION: (LABDEF = COAGULATION-DEFECT .9)
Translate, No further change, or prop name: )
```

```
Rule# or NEW: NEW
RULE015
PREMISE: (DEFPATH IS NOT KNOWN AND ~WNL)
RIJLE015
ACTION: (LABDEF = PLATELET-VASCULAR-DEFCT (.9))

Is WNL a new parameter ? Yes
(in group PATIENT-PARMS)
What kind of parm is WNL -- Yes/no, Singlevalued,
    Multivalued, or Ask-All? Yes/no
WNL
TRANS: (the coagulation screen tests are within normal limits)
WNL
PROMPT: )
PLATELET-VASCULAR-DEFCT -> PLATELET-VASCULAR-DEFECT ? Yes
Translate, No further change, or prop name: )
```

The following 4 rules finally get to use those lab tests defined above.

```
Rule# or NEW: NEW
RULE016
PREMISE: (PT = NORMAL, PTT = NORMAL, PC = NORMAL, BT = NORMAL,
    ... TT = NORMAL, AND FSF = NORMAL)
RULE016
ACTION: (WNL)
Translate, No further change, or prop name: )


Rule# or NEW: NEW
RULE017
PREMISE: (PT=HIGH, PTT=HIGH, TT=HIGH, BT=NORMAL, PC =NORMAL,
    ... FSF = NORMAL)
RULE017
ACTION: (DEFAPTH = MULTIPLE/FIBRIN)
DEFAPTH -> DEFPATH ? Yes
Translate, No further change, or prop name: )


Rule# or NEW: NEW
RULE018
PREMISE: (PT = HIGH, PTT=HIGH, TT=NORMAL, BT=NORMAL,
    ... PC = NORMAL, FSF = NORMAL)
RULE018
ACTION: (DEFPATH = COMMON)
Translate, No further change, or prop name: )


Rule# or NEW: NEW
RULE019
```

PREMISE: *(PT = NORMAL, PTT = HIGH, TT=NORMAL, BT=NORMAL,*
    ... PC=NORMAL, FSF = NORMAL)
RULE019
ACTION: *(DEFPATH = INTRINSIC)*
Translate, No further change, or prop name: ⟩

> *And now a couple of rules to conclude* DX, *a more specific diagnosis of enzymatic or platelet defect.*

Rule# or NEW: NEW
RULE020
PREMISE: *(REASON = BLEEDING-HISTORY, SIGBLEED,*
    ... FINALDEF = COAGULATION-DEFECT AND
    ... DEFPATH = MULTIPLE/FIBRIN)
RULE020
ACTION: *(DX = DXMULTIPLE)*

Is DXMULTIPLE a new member of TEXTAGS ? Yes

> *Here* DXMULTIPLE *appears as a value of the parameter* DX, *but this is slightly different from other values. Since* DX *was defined to take on arbitrary text as value, the parser expects here a piece of text, or a marker for a piece of text. The atom* DXMULTIPLE *is the latter, so a brief diversion is called for here to find out what* DXMULTIPLE *stands for.*

DXMULTIPLE
TRANS: *(DIC, liver disease, congenital hypofibrinogenemia,*
    ... fibrin structural defects, or antithrombin V are consistent
    ... with the patient's bleeding disorder)

[back to RULE020 now]
Translate, Delete, No change, or name of prop to modify: TRANSLATE

RULE020

   If: 1) Bleeding-history is one of the reason for this
           consultation,
        2) There is an episode of significant bleeding in the
           patient,
        3) Coagulation-defect is one of the final blood disorders
           of the patient, and
        4) The defective coagulation pathway of the patient is
           multiple/fibrin
   Then: It is definite (1.0) that the following is one of the
           blood coagulation diagnoses of the patient: DIC,
           liver disease, congenital hypofibrinogenemia, fibrin
           structural defects, or antithrombin V are consistent
           with the patient's bleeding disorder

Translate, Delete, No change, or name of prop to modify: ⟩

```
Rule# or NEW: NEW
RULE021
PREMISE: (REASON = BLEEDING-HISTORY, SIGBLEED,
   ... FINALDEF = COAGULATION-DEFECT AND
   ... DEFPATH = EXTRINSIC)
RULE021
ACTION: (DX = DXVII)
Is DXVII a new member of TEXTAGS ? Yes
DXVII
TRANS: (the patient has a factor VII deficiency)

[back to RULE021 now]
Translate, No further change, or prop name: )


Rule# or NEW: )



Rules, Parms, Go, etc. ? Save
<VANMELLE>CHANGES.;4
```

> *Having reached a "stopping point" of sorts, the designer explicitly saves all the changes made so far.*

```
Rules, Parms, Go, etc. ? Go [confirm] )
```

> *Designer selects the command to run a consultation. What follows is a sample consultation to test this initial rule set, with the designer supplying the answers that would ordinarily be given by the client in a finished consultation program.[6]*

```
Special options (type ? for help):
** )
```

> *Special options include such things as running saved cases from the library, or altering the rule interpreter's printing mode (Section 4.4).*

```
22-Apr-80 21:22:06

--------PATIENT-1--------
1) Name:
** FRED
2) Age:
** 23
3) Sex:
** MALE
4) Race:
** CAUCASIAN
5) Indicate your reason(s) for requesting this consultation:
** BLEEDING-HISTORY
6) Pt:
** 16
```

```
7) Ptt:
** 30
8) Do you believe that the bleeding episode in fred is
   significant?
** Y
```

Designer notes that the patient's name is not capitalized; this will be fixed later.

```
9) What type of bleeding describes fred's most recent episode
   of bleeding?
** HEMARTROSIS
=HEMARTHROSIS
```

Here EMYCIN has applied the spelling corrector, using the expected list of values for this parameter (BLDTYPE).

```
10) Was the onset of bleeding immediate or delayed?
** IMMEDIATE
11) Is there a history of a genetic bleeding disorder in fred's
    family?
** Y
```

```
I was unable to make any conclusion about the final blood
    disorders of fred, whether there is a consistent estimation
    of fred's blood disorder or the blood coagulation diagnoses
    of fred.
```

This is a common outcome for the first test of a knowledge base—no conclusions at all. There may be a break in the inference chain somewhere: a missing rule, or a rule whose conditions were not quite right. The problem now is to locate the error. One method is to have EMYCIN guide the debugging. What follows is a portion of the TEIRESIAS program [Davis 76] adapted to EMYCIN. Other debugging methods are discussed in Section 4.4.

```
Enter Debug/review phase, or other option (? for help) ? Debug/review

                    ***************************

Enter the parameters whose values you wish to review.

Parameter to check: CONSISTENT
```

None of the 3 goal parameters was successfully concluded, but recalling that FINALDEF is dependent on CONSISTENT, the designer selects the latter. The debugger now checks what conclusion, if any, was made, and how it was made or could have been made.

```
I was unable to determine whether there is a consistent
    estimation of fred's blood disorder.

Should it have been possible to conclude about whether there is a
consistent estimation of fred's blood disorder?
** YES
Should it have been possible to conclude that there is a
consistent estimation of fred's blood disorder?
** YES
```

The other possibility, of course, is to conclude that there was no consistent estimation.

```
The following rules could have concluded about:
    the likelihood that there is a consistent estimation of
        fred's blood disorder
Rules 4, 3.
```

The debugger locates the rules that could have made the desired conclusion and examines each to see why the conclusion was not made.

```
RULE004
-------

  If:  1) Clindef = coagulation-defect, and
       2) Labdef = coagulation-defect
  Then:  Consistent = yes (1.0)

Is this rule correct?
** YES
```

The rule might have failed because its premise was incorrect; designer rules out that possibility.

```
Clause 2 of RULE004 {coagulation-defect is one of the blood
    defects of the patient (based on the coagulation screen test
    only)} was already known to be false for PATIENT-1, so the
    rule was never tried.

Should its premise have succeeded when applied to PATIENT-1?
** YES
[Bad clause was "coagulation-defect is one of the blood defects
    of fred (based on the coagulation screen test only)".]
```

At this point the debugger has changed the focus of the problem from why there was no conclusion for CONSISTENT *to determining why the conclusion for* LABDEF *was wrong.*

```
I concluded that the blood defects of fred (based on the
    coagulation screen test only) are: platelet-vascular-defect
    (.9).

Is this entirely correct (i.e., no values are extraneous or
missing)?
** NO
Is the value PLATELET-VASCULAR-DEFECT correct?
** NO
Are any values missing?
** YES
    Which value(s)?
    ** COAGULATION-DEFECT
```

Thus there are two problems: the value concluded (PLATELET-VASCULAR-DEFECT) *was incorrect, and another value* (COAGULATION-DEFECT) *should have been concluded. The debugger starts first with the incorrect conclusion, as that is usually easier to track down.*

RULE015 concluded about:
       the likelihood that platelet-vascular-defect is one of the
       blood defects of fred (based on the coagulation screen
       test only)

Here is the rule that made the incorrect conclusion.

RULE015

  If: 1) Defpath is not known, and
       2) ~wnl
  Then: Labdef = platelet-vascular-defect (.9)

Is this rule correct?
** YES

RULE015 was used to conclude that platelet vascular-detect is one
    of the blood defects of fred (based on the coagulation
    screen test only) (.9). The last question asked before the
    conclusion was made was 7.
Should its premise have failed when applied to PATIENT-1?
** YES
Which clause(s) of the premise were incorrectly true?
** 1

*Debugging has now gone one further level back: the problem now is to
determine why DEFPATH is unknown.*

I was unable to determine the defective coagulation pathway of
    fred.

Should it have been possible to conclude about the defective
coagulation pathway of fred?
** YES
Is there a value that I should have been able to conclude?
** YES
     Which value(s)?
     ** EXTRINSIC
Is there a value that I should have been able to rule out?
** NO

There are no rules which concluded about:
       the likelihood that the defective coagulation pathway of
           fred is extrinsic

Am I missing a rule to conclude that the defective coagulation
pathway of fred is extrinsic?
** YES

*Ah, so it's a case of a missing rule—the designe
failed to write a rule to make this conclusion; as
result, DEFPATH remained unknown and rule 1.
erroneously succeeded.*

Would you like to give me such a rule now?
** YES
Good...

The debugger now invokes the familiar rule editor to allow the designer to enter the desired rule or rules.

```
RULE022
PREMISE: (PT=HIGH, PTT=NORMAL, PC = NORMAL, BT = NORMAL,
    ... TT=NORMAL, FSF=NORMAL)
RULE022
ACTION: (DEFAPTH = EXTRINSIC)
DEFAPTH -> DEFPATH ? Yes
Translate, No further change, or prop name: )

Rule# or NEW: )

[Back to discussing the blood defects of fred (based on the
coagulation screen test only).]
```

Having taken care of one problem, the debugger pops back to the previous level to see if there are any other reasons why LABDEF *was incorrectly concluded.*

```
Am I missing a rule to conclude that platelet-vascular-defect is
not one of the blood defects of fred (based on the coagulation
screen test only)?
** NO

Do you think you have solved the problem with the blood defects
of fred (based on the coagulation screen test only)? (If not, I
will proceed with the values that were missing.)
** YES
```

Designer is satisfied that achieving the correct value for DEFPATH *will allow another rule (Rule014) to correctly conclude* LABDEF. *Debugger pops up one more level to make sure* CONSISTENT *has been handled as well now, and then does some final cleaning up...*

· · ·

```
Do you wish to review the conclusions for any other parameter? No
Do you want to save your work on CHANGES ? Yes
<VANMELLE>CHANGES.;5


I will now re-run the consultation to check the effectiveness of
    your changes. Get comfortable, this may take some time.
```

Actually, on this small rule base it is quite fast.

```
22-Apr-80 21:35:42
[consultation of 22-Apr-80 9:20PM]
```

```
--------PATIENT-1--------
```

The consultation is now rerun silently, with the old questions being answered automatically using the answers supplied the previous time. The change made (the new rule added) has some effect, as the system now asks a few more questions. Note that the first of these is question 12, as the previous 11 questions have already been answered.

```
12) Pc:
** 200000
13) Bt:
** 6
14) Tt:
** 16
15) Fsf:
** ?
```

The "help" response—asks for a rephrasing of the question and an indication of what responses are expected.

```
What is the urea solubility?
Expected responses are: NORMAL or ABNORMAL
Enter HELP for list of user options.
** NORMAL
```

```
The final blood disorders of fred are as follows:
    COAGULATION-DEFECT (.95).

There is a consistent estimation of fred's blood disorder (.51).

The blood coagulation diagnoses of fred are as follows:
    The patient has a factor VII deficiency (.95).
```

Success! This time the correct conclusions were made. Adding rule 22 allowed DEFPATH *to be correctly concluded, which in turn caused rule 15 to fail (it erroneously succeeded last time) and rule 14 to succeed, concluding the correct value for* LABDEF. *That value, together with* CLINDEF *(which was correctly concluded the previous time), allowed rule 4 to succeed, concluding* CONSISTENT, *which in turn succeeded in rules 1 and 2 to conclude* FINALDEF.

```
Enter Debug/review phase, or other option (? for help) ? Parameters
```

There are still a few things to clean up. First, the patient's name was not capitalized...

```
Parameter name: NAME
Subproperty: PROPERNOUN
NAME
PROPERNOUN: ?
```

Help response supplies a piece of canned text describing this property.

The PROPERNOUN property of a parameter, if T, indicates
that the parameter's value should be capitalized in translation.
If the value of this property is the atom ALL, then the
parameter's value will remain in all uppercase.

PROPERNOUN: *T*
Subproperty: *↲*

Parameter name: *↲*

Rules, Parms, Go, etc. ? *Rules*

> *And a second problem—it should have been
> possible to conclude from the value of* BLDTYPE
> *that there was significant bleeding, i.e., question 8
> of the test consultation was redundant. Fix this by
> adding a suitable rule.*

Rule# or NEW: *NEW*
RULE023
PREMISE: *(BLDTYPE = (ONEOF HEMARTHROSIS HEMOPTYSIS HEMATCHESIA
   ... HEMATEMESIS GU-BLEED))*
RULE023
ACTION: *(SIGBLEED)*
Translate, No further change, or prop name: *↲*

Rule# or NEW:

Rules, Parms, Go, etc. ? *Go [confirm] ↲*

> *And now quickly test these two changes...*
Rerun the current consultation? *Yes*

> *Rather than run a new consultation, designer just has the system replay the old
> consultation. The designer does not have to answer any questions this time, as
> they were all answered before.[7]*

22-Apr-80 21:52:15
[consultation of 22-Apr-80 9:20PM]

    --------PATIENT-1--------
    1) Name:
    ** FRED
    2) Age:
    ** 23 YEARS
    3) Sex:
    ** MALE
    4) Race:
    ** CAUCASIAN
    5) Indicate your reason(s) for requesting this consultation:
    ** BLEEDING-HISTORY
    6) Pt:
    ** 15

```
7) Ptt:
** 30
8) Pc:
** 200000
9) Bt:
** 5 MINUTES
10) Tt:
** 15
11) Fsf:
** NORMAL
12) What type of bleeding describes Fred's most recent episode
    of bleeding?
```
                              Note that the patient's name is correct now.
```
** HEMARTHROSIS
13) Was the onset of bleeding immediate or delayod?
** IMMEDIATE
14) Is there a history of a genetic bleeding disorder in Fred's
    family?
** YES
```
                              *And the question about significant bleeding was not
                              asked.*

```
The final blood disorders of Fred are as follows:
    COAGULATION-DEFECT (.95).

There is a consistent estimation of Fred's blood disorder (.51).

The blood coagulation diagnoses of Fred are as follows:
    The patient has a factor VII deficiency (.95).

Enter Debug/review phase, or other option (? for help) ? Quit
```

                              Time to end this session.

```
Do you want to save your work on CHANGES ? Yes
<VANMELLE>CHANGES.;6
```

> EMYCIN *makes sure to clean up before halting. This file of changes will be
> loaded automatically when the designer starts up* EMYCIN *to resume
> construction of this knowledge base. The rules entered above handle only a few
> simple cases; many more rules need to be added and debugged before the
> knowledge base is ready to be used for actual consultations with real cases.*

4

The System-Building Environment

The system designer's principal task is entering and debugging a knowledge base, viz., the rules and the object-attribute structures upon which they operate. This chapter describes the mechanisms in EMYCIN that facilitate that task, loosely labeled "Knowledge Base Construction Aids" in Figure 1-1. These principally concern the entry and editing of rules and associated data structures, but also include debugging aids and other features of EMYCIN that provide a convenient environment for constructing consultation programs.

The level on which the dialogue between system and expert takes place is an important consideration for speed and efficiency of acquisition. The knowledge base must eventually reside in the internal LISP format that the system manipulates to run the consultation, answer questions, and the like. At the very basic level, one could imagine a programmer using the LISP editor to create the necessary data structures totally by hand; here the entire translation from the expert's conceptual rule to LISP data structures is performed by the programmer. At the other extreme, the expert would enter rules in English, with the entire burden of understanding placed on the program.

The actual choice in EMYCIN represents a point between these extremes. Entering rules at the base LISP level is too error-prone, and requires greater facility with LISP on the part of the system designer than is desirable. On the other hand, understanding English rules is far too difficult for a program, especially in a new domain where the vocabulary has not even been identified and organized for the program's use (just recognizing new parameters in free English text is a major obstacle). Thus, the fancy but slow and unreliable mechanisms developed for acquiring MYCIN rules in English were discarded as impractical for use in EMYCIN, and we made the simplifying assumption that the system designer is comfortable with the rule representation and is modestly familiar with very general programming concepts. Within this framework, EMYCIN provides a terse, stylized, but easily understood language for writing rules (termed ARL, see Section 4.1.1), and a high-level knowledge base editor for the knowledge structures in the system. The knowledge base editor performs extensive checks to catch common input errors, such as misspellings, and handles all necessary bookkeeping chores. This allows the system builder to try out new ideas quickly and thereby get some idea of the feasibility of any particular formulation of the domain knowledge into rules.

There are two principal data structures that must be entered: rules and the components of the associative triples upon which they operate. The system designer may enter them in any order that is convenient. They are described in more detail below.

4.1   Rules

Each rule has a unique name (e.g., **RULE005**). The components of a rule are stored on the property list of the rule name as LISP forms, a conjunction of predicates for the *premise* (stored under the indicator **PREMISE**) and one or more conclusions for the *action* (stored under the indicator **ACTION**). In addition, each rule has a **SUBJECT** property, which classifies the rule according to the types of contexts to which it may apply. The rule interpreter uses the **SUBJECT** to determine where in the context tree the rule is applicable.

4.1.1   Abbreviated Rule Language

Although EMYCIN is not equipped to read arbitrary English input, the "language" of associative triples is sufficiently stylized to permit a relief from the raw LISP forms. The abbreviated rule language (ARL) constitutes this intermediate format. ARL is a simplified ALGOL-like language that uses the names of the parameters and their values as operands; the operators correspond to EMYCIN predicates. For example, SACON's Rule 68 shown in Figure 2-1 could have been input or output as:

```
If    Composition = (LISTOF METALS) and
      Error < 5 and
      Nd-stress > .5 and
      Cycles > 10000
Then  Ss-stress = fatigue
```

Figure 4-1. Example of ARL format for rule input/output.

ARL resembles a shorthand form we have seen several of our domain experts use to sketch out sets of rules. The parameter names used are simply the labels that the expert uses in defining the parameters of the domain. The conciseness of ARL makes it much easier to input than English, which is an important consideration when entering a large body of rules.

ARL input is also easy for the program to parse, via a simple precedence parser. Associated with each operator ("**and**," "**=**," etc.) are properties that specify the operator's precedence, and what LISP form the resulting expression should translate into. An operator may behave differently in Premise and Action, in which case two translation forms are associated with the operator. For example, "**=**" translates into (**SAME CNTXT** *op1 op2*) in the Premise, but into (**CONCLUDE CNTXT** *op1 op2* **TALLY** *cf*) in the Action. This parsing information is already supplied for the basic system functions; the system builder may expand the set of operators to include new functions by supplying the necessary properties.[1]

LISP and ARL may be freely intermixed. Standard LISP forms (the expression "**(LISTOF METALS)**" in the example above) may be used as operands to handle expressions for which there is no ARL operator; they remain unchanged in the parsing process. Conversely, ARL forms may appear as LISP forms inside of normal rule clauses.

Rules may also be displayed in ARL, for users who prefer it to the more verbose English translations. The mechanism used is similar to that of normal translation: associated with each predicate function is an ARL translation pattern. Since this pattern has the same form as regular translation patterns, the scheme is reasonably extensible; if a predicate has no ARL translation pattern, its regular one is used.

4.1.2   Rule Checking—Syntax

As each rule is entered or edited, it is checked for syntactic validity to catch common input errors. By "syntactic" we mean concerning the form of the rule—that terms are spelled correctly, values are legal for the parameters with which they are associated, etc.—rather than its information content (i.e., whether the rule "makes sense"). Performing the syntactic check at acquisition time reduces the likelihood that the consultation program will fail due to "obvious" errors, leaving the expert to concentrate on debugging logical (semantic) errors and omissions.

The purely syntactic check is made by comparing each clause with the corresponding function template, and seeing that, for example, each **PARM** slot is filled by a valid parameter, and that its **VALUE** slot is a legal value for the parameter. If an unknown parameter is found, the checker tries to correct it with the INTERLISP spelling corrector, using a spelling list of all parameter in the system. If that fails, it asks if this might be a new parameter, in which case it defines the new parameter and, in a brief diversion, prompts the system builder to describe it. Thus, the expert could just concentrate on entering rules, and never explicitly invoke the parameter editor.[2]

If the checker finds an illegal *value* for a parameter, the action is similar: spelling correction is tried against the list of legal values for the parameter; if that fails, the checker asks if this is a new value, and if so it is added to the appropriate property of the parameter.

Although the **PARM** and **VALUE** slots account for virtually all the checking in a rule that is entered in pure ARL, other slots may also be relevant when arbitrary LISP forms are used, For those slots for which the system has enough information concerning the type of expression that may fill the slot, checks similar to those described above are performed: **CNTXT** must be filled by a valid context variable (usually the variable **CNTXT** itself, but this may be different in mapping rules); **CF** must be filled by a valid certainty factor (a numeric constant in the correct range, or a numeric expression); and, of course, a valid function name must appear in the function position. The case of a missing argument to a function, or arguments appearing out of order, is usually detected as an argument appearing in a slot whose descriptor (**PARM**, **VALUE**, etc.) does not match it.

If the rule checker finds an error it cannot correct it prints a message pointing out the error and puts the designer into the LISP editor to correct the rule. The designer can decline to edit the rule, thereby claiming it is correct as stands (or that the designer is deferring action on it); otherwise the edited rule is passed through the rule checker again.

4.1.3   Rule Checking—Semantics

A limited semantic check is also performed: each new or changed rule is compared with any existing rules that conclude about the same parameter to make sure it does not directly contradict or subsume any of them.[3] A contradiction occurs when two rules with the same set of premise clauses make conflicting conclusions; subsumption occurs when one rule's premise is a subset of the other's, so that the first rule succeeds whenever the second one does (i.e., the second rule is more specific), and both conclude about the same values. While contradiction is always an error, subsumption need not be—the expert may intend that both conclusions be made when the more specific one succeeds (the more specific rule may simply be written to boost the CF of the value concluded in the more general[4]). In either case, the interaction is reported to the expert, who may then examine or edit any of the offending rules.

4.1.4 Rule Bookkeeping

As rules are added or changed, the knowledge base editor automatically updates internal pointers that index the rule according to the parameters it uses. The most important of these is the list of rules that conclude about each parameter, used by the rule interpreter when tracing the parameter (Section 2.2).

Each new rule is also given a **SUBJECT**, which specifies the type(s) of contexts to which it may apply; if the designer is merely editing an old rule, its **SUBJECT** is checked to make sure it is still valid. The rule interpreter uses the **SUBJECT** to determine at runtime whether a rule under consideration can be applied to the current context, whether it must be applied to descendent contexts (see Section 2.6.3.3), or whether the rule is applicable at all. The syntactic constraints on the **SUBJECT** are that (1) all parameters in a rule must belong either to the **SUBJECT** context (the one to which the rule is applied) or to nodes higher in the context tree; and (2) at least one of the parameters belongs to the **SUB-JECT** context, i.e., the rule interpreter should not try to apply the rule any lower in the tree than necessary.

SUBJECT classification can often be performed on a purely syntactic basis. From examination of the parameters used in the rule, the **SUBJECT** classifier can determine where in the context tree the rule may be applicable. The **SUBJECT** need not be uniquely determinable from the rule itself, however (e.g., one of the parameters may be applicable to more than one type of context), so the **SUBJECT** classifier has three possible actions:

(1) The **SUBJECT** is uniquely determined. In this case the classifier simply announces the **SUBJECT**.

(2) There is more than one syntactically legal **SUBJECT**, i.e., it is possible for the rule to apply to more than one type of context. In this case, the classifier lists from the set of defined **SUBJECT**s those that are legal and asks the expert to select one (or confirm it if there is but one). If a syntactically legal **SUBJECT** has not been defined yet, the expert may define (and select) it at this point. Since the system automatically defines a **SUBJECT** for each context type the expert defines, the only time the expert need define a **SUBJECT** is when a rule is to apply to multiple context types.[5]

(3) There is *no* syntactically legal **SUBJECT**, i.e., the designer has constructed a rule that references disjoint parts of the tree. Such a rule is ambiguous in its bind-

ings—the rule interpreter cannot determine for each of the parameters in the rule which context is intended.[6] The rule is thus in error and the designer must fix it, as in other error cases.

To illustrate the three cases, suppose the context hierarchy were as shown in Figure 4-2 below, where there are two types of culture context (**POS-CUL** and **NEGCUL**), only one of which has further descendents.

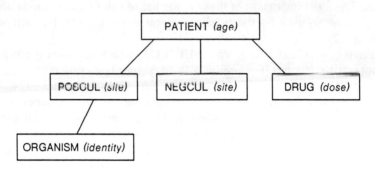

Figure **4-2**. A sample hierarchy of context types. The names in parentheses are sample parameters associated with each type of context; POSCUL and NEGCUL share the same parameter set.

Then,

(1) A rule mentioning the parameters *identity* and *site* could apply to **ORGANISM** contexts only, so the **SUBJECT** would be uniquely determined;

(2) A rule mentioning *site* and *age* could apply to either **POSCUL** or **NEGCUL** contexts, so the designer would have to specify which one (or both) were desired; and

(3) A rule mentioning *identity* and *dose* would be illegal, because the context types with which they are associated (**ORGANISM** and **DRUG**) are not in a strict ancestor/descendent relationship in the hierarchy.

Of course, if the domain has a trivial context tree (only one context type, the root), as was the case with the CLOT example of the previous chapter, then **SUBJECT** classification is also trivial, and is never even explicitly mentioned.

The rule checker, ARL parser, and **SUBJECT** classifier are really all parts of one large rule processor. As the rule is scanned to check for legal parameters and values, the parameter types are collected for the subsequent use of the **SUBJECT** classifier. If an "illegal" LISP form is found that contains ARL operators, it is passed off to the ARL parser.[7]

4.2 The Associative Triples

While one usually thinks of the rules as the principal carrier of "knowledge" in an EMYCIN application, they are, in implementation terms, but one component of the knowledge base. The rules test relationships among, and make conclusions about, the consultation "data"—the associative triples. In order for the rules to operate, the system designer needs to have supplied static properties of the triples: their explicit interconnections, how to ask the client (consultation user) for a piece of data, what values a parameter may take on, etc. Thus, if one views the rules as the "program," then the other component of the knowledge base consists of the declarations and static data structures.

The *contexts* in a particular consultation are organized into the *context tree*, as described in Chapter 2. The system builder supplies both the context types and the static interconnections that determine the structure of the context tree in a consultation. Each context type is described by its position in the static hierarchy (i.e., its parent and offspring context types), an English translation of what it represents (to be used in talking about the context generally), and an indication of which parameters belong to it (to enable the "binding mechanism" of the context tree). In domains where there is no context tree at all, only the root of the degenerate tree (i.e., the central object of the consultation) need be described. In this case, all of the system parameters apply to the root context.

Parameters are simply any "properties" that may be used to describe a context. They are organized into groups according to the types of contexts to which they apply. The system builder describes each parameter by giving it an English translation (e.g., **SITE**: *the site of the culture*), indicating to which context type or types it can belong, and what values it may take on. Further description varies: some information is relevant only to certain kinds of parameters; some is necessary for certain optional system features (e.g., information to give the client in response to a help request about this parameter).

4.2.1 Property Checking

All of the information mentioned above is stored as properties of the context or parameter being described. When a new entity is defined, the acquisition routines automatically prompt for the properties that are always needed; the designer may also enter optional properties (those needed to support special EMYCIN features). For a context or parameter that is already defined, the designer may choose to modify selected properties. In either case, the system is performing several background tasks:

(1) As each property is entered it is checked for syntactic correctness, to the extent that constraints on the properties are known. For example, the translation property **TRANS** of a parameter must satisfy certain assumptions of the rule printer; the **UNITS** property of a numeric-valued parameter must be a valid unit name.

(2) Other data structures affected by this property may be modified, e.g., inverse pointers.

(3) The system may prompt for other properties whose need is suggested by the property just entered; e.g., if the expert says a parameter takes on numeric values (by entering a suitable **EXPECT** property), a **UNITS** property may be called for.

This automatic checking relieves the system builder of much of the burden of remembering all the details that various parts of the EMYCIN system need and helps avoid inadvertent inconsistencies in the knowledge base.

4.2.2   Operation of the Property Checker

The properties mentioned above are checked on entry by comparing their values against a *template* associated with the property itself. The template is a pattern composed of a small set of primitives from the EMYCIN and LISP worlds, e.g., **PARM** and **LIST**, combined into list structures, possibly with conjunctions and disjunctions. The property checker is then a pattern matcher comparing the property's value against the primitives in the template.

If any part of the template is not satisfied, the checker points out the error, together with a translation of the part of the template not satisfied, and drops into the editor to allow the designer to repair the error. It can be forgiving, however, in the manner of the rule checker. For example, if an atom is matched against the template primitive **PARM** and fails, the checker tries spelling correction, and if that, too, fails it asks whether the atom is a new parameter.

Property templates are stored internally as the **PROPFORM** property of the property name. Figure 4-3 shows the template used to check the **INITIALDATA** property (Section 2.6.1.2), along with its translation. If the property checker is given a non-list as the value of the **INITIALDATA** property, it will complain that the entire value is wrong, and print the translation to show what is expected. If given a list, one of whose elements is not a parameter, it will try spelling correction, then ask whether the atom is a new parameter, and failing both, it will print the offending atom, together with the message that it was expecting in that position *"a parameter."* If given a list of parameters, one of which is not marked

ASKFIRST, it will translate just the **SATISFIES** portion of the template in its error message.

INITIALDATA

PROPFORM: (LISTOF (AND PARM (SATISFIES (GETPROP X 'ASKFIRST))))

Translation: *"A list of parameters,*
each of which satisfies (GETPROP ⟨parameter⟩ 'ASKFIRST)"

Figure 4-3. The template used to check the INITIALDATA property, and how that template is translated into English by EMYCIN during interaction with the system designer.

Updating system lists and pointers and prompting for other properties where indicated is accomplished in a similar fashion: they are actions associated with the property being modified. The action may be any LISP form, and it is allowed to examine the atom, property, and value being added or changed. For example, Figure 4-4 shows the action taken when the **EXPECT** property is changed: if the value is one of the markers used to indicate numeric-valued parameters, then the system prompts for the **UNITS** property (which tells the system in what units the value of the parameter is to be stored).

EXPECT

IFCHANGED: (if (MEMB VALUE '(NUMB POSNUMB))
                then (PROMPTFOR UNITS))

Figure 4-4. The action to be performed when the EXPECT property is entered or changed.[8]

4.3   Other Considerations in Knowledge Acquisition

4.3.1   Auxiliary Data Structures

Sometimes rules make use of auxiliary data structures (lists, tables, "grids") that are more compact and/or efficient than expressing the knowledge they embody in rule form. For example, in MYCIN there is a static table of known properties of organisms (gramstain, morphology, etc.). The antecedent rule of Figure 2-8 accesses that table to make conclusions about particular organisms in a consultation. This one rule, with its table, concisely embodies the equivalent of 124 rules (one for each of the organisms known to MYCIN), each of the general form:

```
If:   The identity of the organism is definitely identity

Then: 1) The gramstain of the organism is gram,
      2) The morphology of the organism is morph,
      3) The aerobicity of the organism is air,
      4) The genus of the organism is genus,
```

where the italicized items would be filled with different values corresponding to each organism identity.

Currently, these auxiliary data structures are not well integrated into the knowledge-acquisition routines; the database editor simply treats them as LISP data structures (variables and property lists) that the designer may enter, modify, save, and restore. We hope in the future to provide more extensive support for acquiring and maintaining such structures in a uniform fashion.

4.3.2   Expanding the Set of Predicates

The one rule component not discussed above is the predicate. Most predicates are domain-independent and hence are not usually considered as an aspect of rule acquisition. This is true of all of the basic predicates supplied initially in EMYCIN.[9] However, the set is extensible, using LISP as the programming language to create the predicate and the regular database editor to provide the description necessary to allow its use by the rule mechanisms. The system builder must write the new predicate function (in LISP) and supply an appropriate template (for rule reading) and an English translation form. The interaction shown in Figure 4-5 illustrates how the predicate **GREATEQDEG** could have been added to PUFF using EMYCIN's present knowledge base editor. The predicate is used to compare disease severities expressed as symbolic values; a typical clause and its translation might be:

Figure 4-5. Defining a new predicate.

```
(GREATEQDEG CNTXT DEG_OAD MODERATE)
```

The severity of obstructive airways disease of the patient is greater than or equal to moderate.

Parameter: *GREATEQDEG*

> *A new predicate is entered with the normal knowledge base editor routines as a "pseudo-parameter" in the* FUNCTIONS *group.*

```
Group for new parm GREATEQDEG : FUNCTIONS
```

```
GREATEQDEG does not yet have a function definition; do you want to
define it now? Yes
```

> *The designer could have earlier defined the
> function, or used an existing LISP function, in
> which case this step would be omitted.*

```
** (DEFINEQ (GREATEQDEG (CNTXT PARM DEGREE)
** (IF (MEMB (VAL1 CNTXT PARM)
**         (MEMB DEGREE '(NONE MILD MODERATE
**                     MODERATELY-SEVERE SEVERE)))
**   THEN T ELSE NIL]
```

> *Predicate tests the most highly confirmed degree of
> the parameter against the specified degree in the
> standard scale of degrees.*[10]

```
Adding to CHANGES
```

> *System remembers the definition for later saving on
> file.*

```
GREATEQDEG
TEMPLATE: (CNTXT PARM VALUE)
```

> *The template tells the roles of the arguments, for
> the rule checker and other parts of the system that
> "read" rules.*

```
GREATEQDEG
TRANS: (((2 1)) is greater than or equal to (3))
```

> *Tells how to translate a call to this function.*[11]

4.3.3 Initial Acquisiton Phase

The very first phase of acquisition is of a different nature than the incre-
mental acquisition of rules and parameters described above. The system
builder needs to provide the skeleton on which to hang everything else.
This principally means describing the context tree, as was shown for the
very simple context tree in the example of Chapter 3. To help the designer
through this phase, the system takes the initiative and prompts for the
relevant items. It fills in as much information by default as possible in
order to get things going; the designer can later refine any crude initial
guesses made by the system.

4.3.4 System Maintenance

While the system designer builds up the domain knowledge base as described above, EMYCIN automatically keeps track of the changes that

have been made (new or changed rules, parameters, etc.). The accumulated changes can be saved on a file by the system builder explicitly with a simple command, or else automatically by the system every *n* changes (the frequency of auto-saving can be set by the system builder). When EMYCIN is started in a subsequent session, the system looks for this file of changes and loads it in to restore the knowledge base to its previous state.

EMYCIN also provides an assortment of utility functions, currently accessible from the INTERLISP executive. These utilities allow the designer to examine or manipulate the knowledge base in various ways. For example, the designer can display particular rules or parameters, or make listings of the entire knowledge base or selected subsets of it. Another utility displays the implicit reasoning tree formed by statically backchaining the rules (e.g., Figure 4-6 shows, for the partial knowledge base acquired in Chapter 3, which parameters are used to conclude about which other parameters). An initial version of the dictionary needed for operation of the QA module can be constructed by the system from the words

```
FINALDEF LABDEF DEFPATH PT  NPT
                        PTT NPTT
                        PC  NPC
                        BT  NBT
                        TT  NTT
                        FSF
                 WNL PT  etc.
                     PTT etc.
                     PC  etc.
                     BT  etc.
                     TT  etc.
                     FSF
         CONSISTENT CLINDEF SIGBLEED BLDTYPE
                             BLDTYPE
                             ONSET
                             FAMILY
                    LABDEF etc.
         CLINDEF etc.
```

Figure 4-6. The tree of parameters for the example of Chapter 3. The root of the tree (FINALDEF, one of the goal parameters in CLOT) is on the left; leaves (parameters for which there are no rules) are on the right. Reading left to right, each successive level of the tree shows which parameters are used by the rules that conclude about the parameters in the previous level, e.g., rules that conclude the parameter CONSISTENT use the parameters CLINDEF and LABDEF. The indication "etc." stands for a subtree already displayed earlier in the analysis.

used in the translations of the domain's parameters. Other utilities allow the designer to expand and refine the dictionary by adding synonyms, or by "tuning" the pointers used to associate the English words in a user's questions with domain parameters.

4.3.5 Human Engineering

While the discussion so far has concentrated on the acquisition of the knowledge base, it is also important that the resulting consultation program be pleasing in appearance to its user. EMYCIN's existing human-engineering features relieve the system builder of many of the tedious cosmetic concerns of producing a human-usable program. Since the main mode of interaction between the consultation program and the client is in the program's questions and explanations, most of the features concentrate on making that interface as comfortable as possible. The main feature in this category that has been described so far is the explanation program—the client can readily find out why a question is being asked, or how the program arrived at its conclusions. The designer also has control, by optionally specifying the **PROMPT** for each parameter that is asked, over the manner in which questions are phrased. More detail can be specified, for example, than would appear in a simple prompt generated by the system from the parameter's translation.

4.3.5.1 Terminal Input Facility—TTYIN.
EMYCIN supplies a uniform input facility, called TTYIN. TTYIN permits the normal input editing functions—character, word, and line deletions—and on display terminals allows fancier editing capabilities (insertion or deletion in the middle of the line, for example) in the style of display text editors such as TVEDIT and EMACS. TTYIN performs spelling correction and TENEX-style completion on Altmode from a list of possible answers; most commonly this list is the list of legal values for the parameter being asked about, as supplied by the system designer. Arbitrary tab stops can be specified; this ability enables tabular input format (Section 2.6.1.3).

TTYIN is directly useful to the system builder as well. EMYCIN's knowledge acquisition routines all use it to obtain input, thereby allowing the automatic completions and some of the spelling corrections illustrated in Chapter 3. Since TTYIN also supports general LISP input, those system designers using display terminals in effect have a fancy display editor as their LISP input routine; this has proved to be quite a popular feature. In places where EMYCIN gives a suggested value, it loads TTYIN's buffer with the value and allows the user to edit it or accept it unchanged simply by typing a carriage return. The same sort of procedure is used for editing simple LISP structures, which is a great help to system builders who are not adept at using the INTERLISP editor.

4.3.5.2   Help facilities.   In most places, EMYCIN allows the client to type a question mark to obtain help concerning what is expected or what her options are whenever prompted for input. In the case of the program asking for the value of a parameter, EMYCIN provides simple help in the form of what the legal answers to the questions are, and, if possible, rephrasing the question.[12] The system designer can also include more substantial help by giving rephrasings or elaborations on the original question; these are simply entered via the database editor as an additional property of the parameter in question.[13] Another optional property specifies expected "ambiguous" answers that a client might give to a question about the parameter, and the correct manner in which to resolve them (usually by asking for clarification from among the likely alternatives), which is more helpful to the client than merely learning that her response was not one the system was expecting.

The client may also interrupt at any time to type a comment or gripe, which is automatically mailed to the designated system maintainer.

4.4   The Debugging Process

There is more to building a knowledge base than just entering rules and affiliated data structures. Any errors or omissions in the initial knowledge base must be corrected in the debugging process. In EMYCIN the principal method of debugging is to run sample consultations; i.e., the expert plays the role of the client seeking advice from the system and checks that the correct conclusions are made. The knowledge acquisition facilities described above play a central role in debugging, of course, as the expert modifies existing rules or adds new ones in response to errors detected while testing the knowledge base.

The following sections describe the tools in EMYCIN used to assist in locating errors in the knowledge base.

4.4.1   Explanation System

While the explanation program was designed to allow the consultation user to view the program's reasoning,[14] it is also a helpful high-level debugging aid for the system designer. Without having to resort to LISP-level manipulations, she can examine any inferences that were made, find out why others failed, and thereby locate errors or omissions in the knowledge base. The TEIRESIAS program [Davis 76] developed the **WHY/HOW** capability used in EMYCIN for this very task.

EMYCIN provides a debugger based on a portion of the TEIRESIAS program to actively guide the expert through the program's reasoning chain and locate faulty (or missing) rules (this is illustrated in the brief debugging session of Chapter 3). The debugger starts with a conclusion made during a test consultation that the expert has indicated is incorrect, and follows the inference chain back to locate the error. At any step in the chain, there might be an incorrect or missing conclusion, caused by a rule that incorrectly succeeded, by a rule that failed when it should have succeeded, or by the absence of a rule from the knowledge base. When an error is located, the standard rule editor is invoked to allow the expert to enter a new rule or fix the erroneous one. When the expert is satisfied that the errors have been corrected, the consultation is replayed automatically with the modified knowledge base to see if the desired effect was achieved.

4.4.2 Watching the Rule Interpreter

While the TEIRESIAS-style debugger is useful for methodically tracking down isolated errors in a knowledge base, it may be less appropriate in a knowledge base with large gaps in it, or where the system designer already has a good idea of where the weaknesses lie. To pick out grosser errors in the knowledge base, it is sometimes useful to watch the rule interpreter in action. During an ordinary consultation, of course, the only time the rule interpreter is in evidence is when it asks a question (or the action of some rule performs some visible action, such as displaying a conclusion). However, the rule interpreter has a verbose mode, in which it prints out assorted information about what it is doing: which rules it tries, which succeed (and what conclusions they make), which fail (and for what reason), etc. The information is available in several levels of detail. The following example shows how the test consultation of page 55 would appear when run in this verbose mode.

Figure 4-7. A test consultation demonstrating the play-by-play printout of the rule interpreter's reasoning.

• • •

Picking up following question 5, the last of the INITIALDATA *parameters to be asked...*

```
--[1] Findout: FINALDEF of PATIENT-1
```
Current goal is identified.
```
Trying RULE002/PATIENT-1;
```
Each rule tried and the context to which it is applied is listed.
```
   --[2] Findout: LABDEF of PATIENT-1
Trying RULE015/PATIENT-1;
   --[3] Findout: DEFPATH of PATIENT-1
Trying RULE019/PATIENT-1;
   --[4] Findout: PT of PATIENT-1
Trying RULE009/PATIENT-1;
   6) Pt:
** 16
RULE009 succeeded.
Conclude: PT of PATIENT-1 is HIGH (1.0)
```
Outcome of successful rule is printed.
```
   --[4] Finished: PT of PATIENT-1
```
Finished with subgoal, pop to previous level (3: DEFPATH).
```
RULE019 failed due to clause 1
```
Reason for failure of a rule is noted.
```
Trying RULE018/PATIENT-1;
   --[4] Findout: PTT of PATIENT-1
Trying RULE010/PATIENT-1;
   7) Ptt:
** 30
RULE010 succeeded.
Conclude: PTT of PATIENT-1 is NORMAL (1.0)
   --[4] Finished: PTT of PATIENT-1
RULE018 failed due to clause 2
RULE017 failed {in preview} due to clause 2
   --[3] Finished: DEFPATH of PATIENT-1
   --[3] Findout: WNL of PATIENT-1
RULE016 failed {in preview} due to clause 1
   --[3] Finished: WNL of PATIENT-1
RULE015 succeeded.
Conclude: LABDEF of PATIENT-1 is PLATELET-VASCULAR-DEFECT (.9)
RULE014 failed {in preview} due to clause 1
   --[2] Finished: LABDEF of PATIENT-1
   --[2] Findout: CONSISTENT of PATIENT-1
RULE004 failed {in preview} due to clause 2
Trying RULE003/PATIENT-1;
   --[3] Findout: CLINDEF of PATIENT-1
Trying RULE008/PATIENT-1;
   --[no rules to conclude SIGBLEED of PATIENT-1]
```
No rules to conclude this parameter, so a question is asked.
```
   8) Do you believe that the bleeding episode in fred is
      significant?
** Y
   9) What type of bleeding describes fred's most recent episode
      of bleeding?
** HEMARTHROSIS
   --[no rules to conclude BLDTYPE of PATIENT-1]
```

```
RULE008 failed due to clause 2
Trying RULE007/PATIENT-1; RULE007 succeeded.
Conclude: CLINDEF of PATIENT-1 is COAGULATION-DEFECT (.3)
Trying RULE006/PATIENT-1;
    10) Was the onset of bleeding immediate or delayed?
    ** IMMEDIATE
RULE006 failed due to clause 2
Trying RULE005/PATIENT-1;
    11) Is there a history of a genetic bleeding disorder in fred's
        family?
    ** Y
RULE005 succeeded.
Conclude: CLINDEF of PATIENT-1 is COAGULATION-DEFECT (.51)
    --[3] Finished: CLINDEF of PATIENT-1
RULE003 failed due to clause 1
    --[2] Finished: CONSISTENT of PATIENT-1
RULE002 failed due to clause 2
RULE001 failed {in preview} due to clause 2
    --[1] Finished: FINALDEF of PATIENT-1
    --[1] Findout: DX of PATIENT-1
RULE021 failed {in preview} due to clause 3
RULE020 failed {in preview} due to clause 3
    --[1] Finished: DX of PATIENT-1

I was unable to make any conclusion about the final blood
    disorders of fred, whether there is a consistent estimation
    of fred's blood disorder or the blood coagulation diagnoses
    of fred.
```

If the printout indicates that a rule succeeded that should have failed, or vice versa, the expert can interrupt immediately, rather than waiting for the end of the consultation to do a more formal TEIRESIAS-style review. Once the problem is corrected, the expert can then restart and try again, with the consultation automatically replayed up to the point of interruption, only this time with the new/modified rules being used.

4.4.3   Piece-wise Debugging

It is sometimes convenient to construct and debug a knowledge base in pieces, working only on the rules for a particular goal or set of goals at one time. The modularity of the knowledge base makes this quite feasible. If the system designer has not yet written rules to conclude about a particular parameter, then when that parameter is traced during a test consultation, the rule interpreter will find there are no rules to try, and will prompt for the value of the parameter. If the parameter is one that ordinarily would not be asked (i.e., the designer supplied no **PROMPT** for it), EMYCIN asks if it should temporarily prompt for it. Thus, for the purposes of testing selected parts of the knowledge base in a consultation, the expert can supply values for parameters for which she will later write rules.

4.4.4   Case Library

EMYCIN has facilities for maintaining a library of sample cases. These can be used for testing a complete system, or for debugging a growing one. The answers given by the consultation user to all the questions asked during the consultation are simply stored away, indexed by their context and parameter. When a library case is rerun, the answer to each question is looked up and automatically supplied; any new questions resulting from changes in the rule base are asked in the normal fashion. This makes it easy to check the performance of a new set of rules on a "standard" case.[15] It is especially handy during an intensive debugging session, since the expert can make changes to the knowledge base and, with a minimum of extra typing, test those changes—effectively reducing the "turnaround time" between modifying a rule and receiving consultation feedback.

4.4.5   Batch Program

A problem common to most large systems is that the debugging process often introduces new bugs; cases that once ran successfully now fail. To simplify the task of keeping the knowledge base consistent with cases that are known to be correctly solved, EMYCIN's *Batch* program permits the system designer to run any or all cases in the library in background mode. Batch reports back whether any changes in the "results" of the consultation occurred, and invokes the QA module to explain why they occurred. The system builder need only indicate to the system which parameters represent the results or important intermediate steps of the consultation by which the "correctness" of the consultation may be judged. The use of the Batch program could be viewed as a form of semantic checking to supplement the syntactic checking routinely performed at the time of rule acquisition.

4.5   Comparison with TEIRESIAS

The TEIRESIAS program [Davis 76] was another effort at acquiring knowledge from an expert in the form of MYCIN rules and data structures. From the TEIRESIAS work come several of the features in the current EMYCIN implementation: Preview, Unitypath, Metarules, and the **HOW/WHY** explanation facility. However, on the topic of knowledge acquisition, TEIRESIAS and EMYCIN have quite different methods and goals.[16]

TEIRESIAS attempts to carry on the dialogue with the expert entirely in English, with as little as possible reference to the underlying representation and control structure other than to assume the *rule* as the basic unit of knowledge. EMYCIN takes the position that English input is difficult and slow to parse reliably, and that the expert really needs to have more familiarity with the system in order to write rules effectively. In return, EMYCIN grants speed and ease of use. ARL is much easier and quicker for the expert to type than English, while still being "natural" enough for easy comprehension. The parameter names in an ARL expression, for example, are names selected by the expert and therefore likely to be reasonably mnemonic.

TEIRESIAS also takes on a different task. It assumes that a well-established knowledge base already exists (the MYCIN knowledge base in this case), and that the expert wants to debug or add to that knowledge base. As a result, the vocabulary of the domain is already established, making it at least feasible for the program to accept natural language input, and the general structure of the rules is known. From that structure, TEIRESIAS can build *rule models* that provide expectations regarding any new rules to be entered, under the assumption that the new rules will have a form comparable to those already in the system. In addition, TEIRESIAS focuses on acquiring rules within the context of an error; that confined setting makes it easier for the expert to write the rule, and it supplies further expectations to the system to guide the parsing of new rules.

EMYCIN, on the other hand, concentrates more on acquiring a knowledge base from scratch. The domain vocabulary is not yet known to the program, so parsing English is infeasible. Identifying new parameters in free text is difficult enough, in fact, that TEIRESIAS does not even attempt it—TEIRESIAS instead requires the expert to explicitly delimit phrases in the English input that refer to new parameters or values.

EMYCIN and TEIRESIAS do some of the same sorts of rule checking, e.g., making sure that values are legal for the parameters with which they are associated. In EMYCIN, a parameter's list of legal values constitutes a spelling list against which to correct, if necessary, the value supplied by the expert. In TEIRESIAS, the fact that a particular value is associated with a parameter is used to select among alternative parses of a sentence in which the words individually suggest more than one possible parameter. Some other checking is implicit in the act of parsing an English rule; e.g., TEIRESIAS only produces valid parameters in the course of parsing. The analogy to EMYCIN's discovering an invalid parameter in a LISP or ARL clause would be the case of TEIRESIAS failing to parse, or parse correctly, an English clause.

The *templates* used by EMYCIN's property checker are similar in nature to TEIRESIAS's *schemata*, describing the expected form of a data structure and providing information to aid the updating of the necessary data structures. The schemata provide a more general, declarative framework, however, for guiding the acquisition of new primitives, a task which is accomplished in EMYCIN (for new parameters and values) by specialized procedures.

5

The Rule Compiler

The process of *compilation* is used to transform a convenient, human-manipulable representation into one more suited for machine use. The most familiar case is that of programming languages, where compilation either constitutes a prerequisite to machine execution, or, as in languages with interpreters (e.g., LISP), results in much more efficient execution. EMYCIN's production rule "language" also benefits from compilation.

One objection often made to the use of production rules in practice is that they are slow as compared to other representations that are geared more toward performance, such as decision trees. Not only must the rules be "interpreted," but much of the computation performed by the EMYCIN rule interpreter is redundant. For example, if a block of 50 rules all contain the same first clause, that clause will still be evaluated 50 times, as the interpreter does not (and cannot efficiently) carry information about the evaluation of one rule on to the rest.[1] Furthermore, as the rule set grows, a greater proportion of the system's time is spent in the rule interpreter,[2] and the redundant computation can become more of an obvious burden.

The EMYCIN rule compiler (RCOMPL) takes advantage of knowledge available from a static analysis of the rule set (e.g., that a block of rules has a common clause) to produce a more efficient representation. Specifically, it constructs a LISP program that embodies a particular block of rules, but in which redundant computation of related premise clauses is eliminated. The resulting program is an efficient decision tree, which effectively tries several rules in parallel; a single test in the compiled program (e.g., "what is the infection?") can cause a large set of rules to fail at once. RCOMPL then uses the standard LISP compiler to produce machine code. Executing the resulting code is equivalent, in a way stated more precisely later (Section 5.3.1), to interpreting the original rules, but is much faster.[3]

The rule compiler thus allows the consultation program to use an efficient deductive mechanism, even as the rule base expands, while the flexible rule format is still available for acquisition, explanation, and debugging.

5.1 Rules as Program

The list of rules that make conclusions about a particular parameter implicitly constitutes a program to conclude the parameter. According to the operation of EMYCIN's rule interpreter, that program is trivial; the rules are simply interpreted one at a time. If the premise of a rule is true, its action is evaluated. As noted above, if the rules have a common clause, the clause is still evaluated once per rule.

The interpretation of a single rule

$$Premise \Rightarrow Action$$

can be represented simply as the "program"

(if *premise* **then** *action*).

Since ordinarily EMYCIN evaluates *all* of the rules in the list (disregarding for now the case where evaluation stops when the answer is found with certainty), the resulting program for the set of rules would be a series of such conditionals, one for each rule. However, if there are clauses common to more than one premise, they can be factored out, leaving a simpler program. For example, given rules

$$A \text{ and } B \Rightarrow X, \quad A \text{ and } \sim B \Rightarrow Y, \quad \sim A \text{ and } C \Rightarrow Z,$$

the program would be

> **(if** *A*
>   **then (if** *B* **then** *X* **else** *Y*)
>   **else (if** *C* **then** *Z*)),

or the following decision tree:

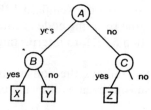

The tree makes exactly two tests to resolve the three rules, making one of three conclusions (X, Y, Z) or falling through with no action.

If there are many common clauses in the rule set, i.e., if a large number of the combinatorially possible conjuncts of the set of clauses are actually represented in the rule set, the branching factor in the decision tree will be high, and the optimization will be greater. Rules sparsely covering a parameter will benefit less from the extraction of common clauses.[4]

5.2 Basic Algorithm

The general strategy for converting a set of rules into a decision tree is shown in Figure 5-1. Note the recursion in Steps 5 and 6. At each level of recursion the procedure is producing a branch of the resulting decision tree, splitting the rule set into smaller rule sets with simpler premises. The first part of the procedure is the terminating condition: eventually a rule's premise becomes empty when all of its clauses have been tested, and its conclusion can then be made at that point in the tree.

Compile[*ruleset*]:

> For all R in *ruleset* for which the premise is now empty (true), **do**
>> (1) output conclusion of R;
>> (2) remove R from *ruleset*.

> **while** *ruleset* is **non-empty do**
>> (3) Select a clause C from the premise of some rule;
>> (4) Output a branch, using clause C as the conditional;
>> (5) On the true side of the branch:
>>> Compile all rules that contain clause C, after removing C from each;
>> (6) On the false side of the branch:
>>> Compile all rules that contain the clause $\sim C$, after removing $\sim C$ from each;
>> (7) Remove from *ruleset* those rules compiled in (5) and (6).

Figure 5-1. The Rule Compiler Algorithm

In cases where the **while** loop executes no more than once at each level (i.e., in each subdivided rule set the selected branch clause or its negation appears in every rule), the resulting structure is a true tree, where each leaf is the conclusion of a rule or "falls through," i.e., takes no action. In such a tree, no more than one rule can succeed at once.[5] More commonly, however, multiple rules may succeed simultaneously, and the resulting structure is a tree of trees, in which the leaves of one subtree (corresponding to one pass through the **while** loop) all fall through to the root of the next subtree. For example, Figure 5-2 depicts a simple case of four rules that conclude values *X1* through *X4* for some parameter. After clause *A* is selected for the first branch, only two rules can be compiled in one tree; the remaining two rules are compiled into a second tree, which logically follows *all* the leaves of the first tree, whether a conclusion was made there or not.

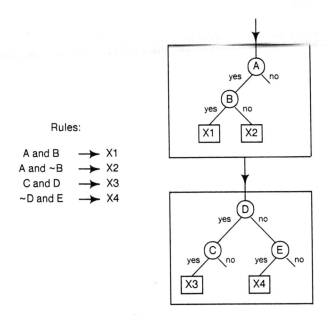

Rules:

A and B   → X1
A and ~B   → X2
C and D   → X3
~D and E   → X4

Figure 5-2. Example of two decision trees in series produced by **Compile** when the rules are not mutually exclusive.

5.2.1   Some Assumptions

The Rule Compiler makes two fundamental assumptions to allow it to build a decision tree out of rules:

(1) *Any given clause always returns the same value, independent of how often it is evaluated; and*

(2) *The order of evaluation of rules within a block is irrelevant.*

The first condition is necessary because in the course of trying a set of rules, a given clause might be evaluated several times by the rule interpreter, but possibly only once in the compiled code. If (1) did not hold, the concept of a decision tree would not even be applicable; it would be something like having the sense of a branch in the tree spontaneously change while control was beneath the branch.

Condition (2) is necessary so that a branch can be extracted from several rules, even if those rules are not consecutive rules in the block. Failure of Condition (2) means that the rules contain more information than is explicitly stated in them, viz., that the truth of a given rule is dependent on the fact that the rules that precede it have already been tested, as is the case in some other production systems (e.g., PSG [Newell 73]).

Fortunately, EMYCIN satisfies these constraints. Condition (2) is explicitly satisfied. Condition (1) holds by virtue of EMYCIN's parameter tracing mechanism. When a parameter's value is not known, it is "traced" (see Section 2.2); thereafter, any reference to the parameter will return the same value.[6] In other words, once it is traced, it is known "forever." Different evaluations of a clause might thus have different side effects (the first evaluation may cause tracing), but the value returned remains constant.

5.2.2   Selecting the Branch Clause

The selection of the branch clause in Step 3 of the **Compile** algorithm is incompletely specified. The only constraint imposed on its selection derives from an ordering convention of the rule interpreter: a rule's clauses are evaluated in the order written. This convention gives the system designer some explicit control over the order in which parameters are traced and/or asked. One of its primary uses is to permit "screening" clauses— generally clauses that prevent "silly" questions from being asked. This is comparable to the convention in many programming languages of "conditional Booleans"—in a form such as "*A* **and** *B*," *A* is tested first, and if false then *B* is not even examined, thereby allowing *A* to screen *B* for exceptional conditions, such as divide by zero.

In order to maintain logical consistency between the source and compiled rules, then, the constraint on clause selection is that a clause of a rule may not be selected as a branch (evaluated) until every preceding clause in the rule is known to be true. However, a clause may be selected if its truth value may be established without side effects, since that is what the ordering convention protects against (the side effect of asking an inappropriate question). In more specific terms, the clause must either

(a) be the first remaining clause in a rule (or equivalently, trace only parameters that are traced in the first clause of *some* rule in the set), or (b) test only parameters that are known to be traced already, e.g., the conclusion parameter in a self-referencing rule, or one of the **INITIAL-DATA** parameters of some context.

Within this ordering constraint, the choice of branch clause does not affect the logical correctness of the compiled code, but it may influence its efficiency. The choice currently employed by RCOMPL is the fairly obvious one of selecting a clause that affects the most rules, i.e., for which the clause or its negation appears in the most rules. The motivation for this choice is twofold; testing the clause in some sense reveals the most "information" about the rules in the set, and testing the most frequent clauses early in the tree reduces the chances that they will have to be tested in multiple places. With regard to the latter consideration, note that selecting the branch clause may partition the rule set into two or three subsets, each having its own tree (or set of trees). If the partition is such that a clause *A* or its negation appears in more than one of the subsets, then a test for *A* will have to appear at least once in each of the trees resulting from those subsets; whereas if *A* had been selected as the branch clause, only one test for it is needed. Since, other things being equal, clauses that appear frequently are more likely to be split up in this fashion, it is desirable to compile the frequent clauses early in the tree.

This choice of branch clause may have a side effect on question order during the consultation: the system will tend to ask the most "reasonable" question out of the unasked clauses in the rule set—most reasonable in that it provides the most information toward the evaluation of the rule set.[7]

5.2.3 Further Refinement

The **Compile** algorithm outlined above speaks only of clauses and their negations. While it is true that many clauses appear in strictly opposite pairs (differing only in the predicate name, e.g., **SAME/NOTSAME, GREATERP*/LESSEQ***), some logically overlap. For example, suppose the branch clause *C* were "**SITE** ~ = **BLOOD**," and some other rule contained the clause *C'* = "**SITE** ~ = (**ONEOF BLOOD SPUTUM**)." *C'* is not identical to *C* or the negation of *C*, and hence the simple algorithm would ignore it. However, *C'* does imply *C* (if the site is neither blood nor sputum, it is in particular not blood), so it is correct to include the rule containing *C'* on the true side of the branch.

In other words, if *C'* is true, then the true side of the branch under *C* will always be followed; there is no sense testing *C'* in any case where the false branch is taken. Furthermore, it may be possible to simplify *C'* using the information that *C* is true; in the example above, *C'* could be simplified to "**SITE** ~= **SPUTUM**," since it is already known that the site is not blood.

Figure 5-3 shows the revision to the **Compile** algorithm that results from taking into account implications between clauses. On the true side of the branch (Step 5) are placed all the rules containing *C*, plus any rule whose truth requires *C*. The simplification step of removing *C* from *C'* means removing the clause altogether when *C* = *C'* (the original Step 5); otherwise, if *C'* is a conjunction of *C* and another expression, then *C* can be removed from the conjunction. Often it is not possible to simplify *C'*; e.g., if *C* = "**AGE** < **12**," no simplification can be made to *C'* = "**AGE** < **6**." However, it is still worth including *C'* under branch *C* as long as *C* is being tested anyway—doing so restricts the number of cases under which *C'* will be tested. A similar procedure is followed for the false side of the branch in Step 6.

Compile[*ruleset*]:

> For all *R* in *ruleset* for which the premise is now empty (true), **do**
>> (1) output conclusion of *R*;
>> (2) remove *R* from *ruleset*.
>
> **while** *ruleset* is non-empty **do**
>> (3) Select a clause *C* from the premise of some rule;
>> (4) Output a branch, using clause *C* as the conditional;
>> (5) On the true side of the branch:
>>> Compile all rules that contain <u>a clause *C'* that implies</u> *C*,
>>> after <u>simplifying *C'* by removing *C* if possible</u>;
>> (6) On the false side of the branch:
>>> Compile all rules that contain <u>a clause *C'* that implies</u> ~*C*,
>>> after <u>simplifying *C'* by removing ~*C* if possible</u>;
>> (7) Remove from *ruleset* those rules compiled in (5) and (6).

Figure 5-3. The Rule Compiler Algorithm, revised to take advantage of clauses with some logical overlap.

In the domains studied so far, a large number of the rules have clauses that do not fall into simple true-false pairs. Thus, RCOMPL needs a simple inference mechanism to get the most out of factoring such clauses (Section 5.2.5).

Note that, under this scheme, a rule containing a clause implied *by* the branch clause cannot be compiled in Step 5. While the clause would certainly succeed on the true side of the branch (it would not have to be tested at all there), that is not the only place that the rule could be reached in the decision tree—the clause might be true as well in cases where the false branch is taken, and thus it would be necessary to compile the rule in two places. This would almost certainly result in a larger program; effect on the execution speed would depend on the probabilities of the branch succeeding.

5.2.4   Uncertainty

Every branch in a conventional decision tree is strictly binary: either the condition is true or false, so only one of the two branches is followed, and any conclusion reached is definitely valid. It is thus difficult to write decision trees for a problem in which some information or reasoning step is uncertain. RCOMPL faces this difficulty in converting rules into decision trees, since clauses in EMYCIN rules are not simply true or false, but return certainty factors (CF's). The **$AND** that joins the clauses in each rule premise is not a simple logical conjunct, but rather accumulates the minimum CF of the premise clauses and uses that minimum to modify the certainty of the conclusion.

The fact that every branch in the final machine code to be produced must be purely binary, even when the conditions tested are not, is reflected in the **Compile** algorithm as already stated. What would be mutually exclusive conditions in a world free of uncertainty (and hence conditions that would fall on opposite sides of a binary branch) may be tested serially in RCOMPL's decision tree—each condition tested in a separate pass of the main **while** loop. For example, the conditions *the identity of the organism is E.coli* and *the identity of the organism is Pseudomonas* can both be true (with some associated CF), and thus if these conditions appeared in two rules, *both* rules would have to be tried. This matter will be discussed further in connection with the inference mechanism (Section 5.2.5).

Propagating the certainty of the premise of a rule to its conclusion is handled by a simple extension to the **Compile** algorithm outlined above. When a rule is interpreted, the minimum CF of the clauses in its premise is accumulated in a variable **TALLY**, which is then passed to the conclusion. To preserve this behavior when a set of rules is compiled, each branch in the resulting tree carries a CF, which is the minimum CF of the clauses evaluated up to that point. Thus, Steps 5 and 6 of **Compile** should also include a statement such as "on the true (false) side of the branch, rebind **TALLY** to be the minimum of **TALLY** and the CF of the clause (negation of clause) just evaluated."

Not every clause returns a CF that affects **TALLY**, however. In fact, only a few predicates ever return CF's other than 1. When the branch clause is a predicate known to always return 1 when true, **TALLY** obviously need not be rebound, since **min**[**TALLY**,1] = **TALLY**. RCOMPL uses information about the value returned by a predicate (e.g., that it always returns **T** or **NIL**, or 1 or 0) to generate more compact and efficient code where possible. Such information is already supplied for the basic EMYCIN predicates; it can be readily added by the system builder for user-defined predicates.

Furthermore, there are a number of parameters that are always known with certainty, e.g., the site of the culture in MYCIN. So even though the predicate **SAME** in general can return any CF, it is known that the clause **(SAME CNTXT SITE anything)** always returns 1 or 0, and thus the remarks about not rebinding **TALLY** also apply here. If the designer informs RCOMPL of these "definite-valued" parameters (by adding a property **DEFVALUED** to the parameter's definition), it can produce better code (see Section 5.2.5).

Note that the mechanism outlined above for handling CF's is not strictly dependent on EMYCIN's implementation, but assumes only that **$AND**'s certainty factor combiner (currently **min**) is a commutative binary operation, so that partial results can be carried down branches of the tree. The computation can be omitted for clauses that return the operation's identity element (in this case, 1).

5.2.5   *The Inference Mechanism*

Even if RCOMPL knew nothing about the logical relationships among clauses in rules, the **Compile** algorithm would still accomplish one useful task: it could factor identical clauses out of a set of rules, thereby eliminating some redundant computation. However, to make best use of the algorithm, RCOMPL needs to be able to infer the logical relationship between any two clauses; specifically, it needs to determine whether one clause is the negation of another (for Step 6), and whether one clause implies another (for the refinement described in Section 5.2.3). Additionally useful would be the ability to simplify clauses, as called for in the modified Step 5 (or 6). And for efficient handling of CF's, RCOMPL needs to know what type of value a clause returns.

The inference mechanism in RCOMPL is fairly simple, but powerful enough to correctly handle the common cases. It knows about the Booleans **and**, **or**, **not**, and DeMorgan's law relating them. Beyond that, it knows of the semantics of individual predicate functions via specified properties of the functions. As usual, the properties are supplied for the basic EMYCIN predicates, and the system builder can easily add the properties for any new predicates specific to an application. In using these properties, RCOMPL attempts only to establish connections between clauses that either test the same parameter/context pair or have the same argument list. This restriction keeps the search for related clauses well confined.

For direct implications, there are two basic assertions about the predicates that can be stated: (1) one predicate function implies another when they have the same arguments, and (2) one clause implies another when certain conditions on the arguments are satisfied. For negation, one can state either that one function is the direct negation of another, or that one function implies the negation of another. By combining these primitives by simple transitivity, RCOMPL can make most of the useful connections. For example, if fn1 $\Rightarrow$ fn2 and fn2 $\Rightarrow$ fn3, then fn1 $\Rightarrow$ fn3; if fn1[x,y,z] $\Rightarrow$ fn2[p,q,r] and fn2 $\Rightarrow$ fn3, then fn1[x,y,z] $\Rightarrow$ fn3[p,q,r].

To show how these connections can be expressed, here are the properties supplied in EMYCIN for the ubiquitous predicate **SAME** (the ARL operator "="), which tests the value of a parameter of a context to see if it is a specified value, or one of a set of values:

SAME

RETURNS:	CF	*This tells* RCOMPL *that* SAME *returns a* CF; *this affects code generation.*
NEGATION:	NOTSAME	SAME *and* NOTSAME *are negations of each other.*
IMPLIES.FN:	(MIGHTBE)	*For a given argument list,* SAME *implies the function* MIGHTBE.
IMPLIES.OTHER:		

This property lists related clauses that may be implied by a SAME *clause; each entry is a pair (function condition), where the condition may examine the values being tested in the two clauses[8] or the parameter itself.*

((KNOWN T)

If SAME *is true, then* KNOWN *is true (i.e.,* SAME *can only be satisfied when the parameter is known).*

(SAME (VSUBSETP P1 Q1))

If SAME *is true for some value or set of values, then it is also true for a superset of those values (P1 and Q1 are the value arguments appearing in the two clauses P and Q being tested for P $\Rightarrow$ Q).*

[DEFNOT (AND (VDISJOINTP P1 Q1)
             (PARMTYPE? PARM 'DEFVALUED])

If P1 and Q1 are disjoint values or sets of values, and the parameter is definite-valued, then if the parameter's value is (in) P1 it definitely is not (in) Q1.

The last entry also illustrates how the inference mechanism is able to take into account some domain-specific information, in this case the knowledge that certain parameters are definite-valued, i.e., are always known with certainty. While, in general, the truth of the clause (**SAME CNTXT parm valu1**) implies nothing about (**SAME CNTXT parm valu2**), if the parameter is definite-valued, these two clauses are mutually exclusive: if a branch is made on one of them, then the other can go on the false side of the branch.[9]

The simplification in Steps 5 and 6 to "remove" the branch clause from the clauses that imply it requires the ability to recognize conjunctions. That is, RCOMPL is using the logic rule

$$A \Rightarrow [(A \text{ and } B) \equiv B]$$

to eliminate some redundant computation when the clause "*A* and *B*" appears under branch *A*. Explicit conjunctions (those written with the function **and**) are, of course, easily recognized, but RCOMPL also has some built-in knowledge that certain predicates are implicit conjunctions. The latter are those functions that behave like conjunctions when given a list of values to test. The most common is the function **NOTSAME**; the clause

(**NOTSAME CNTXT parm (ONEOF value1 value2 . . . valueN))**

is interpreted to mean

(**NOTSAME CNTXT parm value1) and**
(**NOTSAME CNTXT parm value2) and**
. . .   **and**
(**NOTSAME CNTXT parm valueN).**

The simplification in the example of Section 5.2.3 is handled in this manner.

5.2.6   Other Optimization Mechanisms

A simple form of common subexpression elimination is performed on the intermediate LISP program before it is passed to the LISP compiler. The eliminator scans the program in evaluation order, and notes whenever a form to be evaluated has already been evaluated on the path to this point and is still valid. It then sets a temporary variable to the first occurrence of the expression, and replaces the later occurrences with the variable.

As in conventional optimizers, a temporary variable can be reused if the last occurrence of one expression precedes the first occurrence of the next; when the ranges overlap, a new temporary must be generated.

The subexpression eliminator typically helps make more efficient the evaluation of related clauses that are not strict negations. The clauses contain common subexpressions, either explicitly or implicitly (discovered by the inference mechanism). For example, in MYCIN the clauses

(SAME CNTXT SITE BLOOD)
(SAME CNTXT SITE URINE)
(SAME CNTXT SITE CSF)

(which test for the site of the culture being one of three possible values) need not all be evaluated in full. Since the parameter **SITE** is known to be definite-valued, each **SAME** clause is compiled in the form

(VAL1 CNTXT SITE) = *value*,

and the subexpression eliminator simply extracts the **(VAL1 CNTXT SITE)**[10] from each occurrence. This avoids the need to repeatedly look up the value of the parameter **SITE** for each test.

The INTERLISP compiler, of course, has no way of doing such optimization, since it cannot in general make the assumptions that RCOMPL can about lack of side effects. However, this subexpression eliminator has its own limitations. In particular, it knows nothing about loops (which arise from the expansion of mapping rules), and it is unable to extract common subexpressions from both sides of a branch (a space, rather than time optimization), due to the ordering constraint on clauses.

The second major optimization is the elimination of the standard search up the context tree performed by the rule interpreter to determine which context a particular parameter references. This "binding mechanism" is ordinarily invoked for each context/parameter pair used by a predicate. This is another example of information available at compile time: RCOMPL knows what parameters belong with which types of context, so it can determine once, on entering the block, the specific ancestors of the present context needed by *all* the parameters used in the block, eliminating the slow lookup procedure that would otherwise be performed for each parameter encountered.[11]

5.3   Other Considerations

5.3.1   Equivalence to Interpreted Rules

Executing the code produced by RCOMPL is *logically* equivalent to interpreting the same rules. That is, both will produce the same conclusions.

They are not necessarily procedurally equivalent, however. In particular, the two methods may generate questions during the consultation in a different sequence, since the order of evaluation of the rules may be different. However, the order of questions in the compiled code is always directly equivalent to *some* order of evaluation of the original rules, and since the order of the rules for any one parameter is arbitrary, this is acceptable.

Procedural equivalence breaks down still further once one considers the embellishments to the basic rule interpreter algorithm discussed in Section 2.6. These are discussed further below (Section 5.5).

5.3.2　Managing **SUBJECT** *Information*

Each rule has a **SUBJECT** specifying the types of contexts to which the rule can be applied (Section 4.1.4). It is not necessary that all rules in a single **UPDATED-BY** list have the same **SUBJECT**; hence RCOMPL cannot necessarily compile all the rules into one block, since the block must have a single **SUBJECT**.

The current implementation of RCOMPL does the obvious thing: it breaks the list into groups of rules having a common **SUBJECT**, and compiles each group as an independent block of the same **SUBJECT**. The output of the compiler is then a list of one or more blocks. A fair efficiency gain is still realized here, as the monitor now need only check the **SUBJECT** once for an entire block of rules, rather than for each component rule (as it does when interpreting the rules).

A more sophisticated implementation might choose to view the **SUBJECT** as simply another premise clause that appears first in all the rules, is always known and causes no tracing—simply another clause to branch on (possibly not even the top-level branch, although it seems likely that it would be so). This approach is possible if the multiple **SUBJECT**'s chosen are all at the same syntactic level in the tree; the **SUBJECT** of the resulting block would be the "least common denominator" of all those in the group.

5.3.3　Premature Termination

The rule interpreter ordinarily stops as soon as the parameter it is trying to find out becomes known with certainty. To mimic that behavior in the compiled code, RCOMPL must generate code along with each conclusion to test whether the conclusion just made should terminate the block immediately. Actually, RCOMPL is a little smarter than that: it generates said code only when termination *might* occur. There are several cases:

(1) The parameter being traced is multivalued. Termination cannot occur in this case, because knowing one value with certainty does not exclude others; hence, no extra code is generated.

(2) The conclusion is being made with a CF other than 1.0, as determined by "reading" the conclusion via its template. Termination cannot occur here, either. Regardless of the certainty of the premise, if the parameter was not known with certainty before this conclusion, it still is not. Thus, no extra code is generated.

(3) The CF in the conclusion is 1.0. In this case, the rule *might* exit:

(a) If the premise is known to be definite at compile time, i.e., no CF computation is needed to compile the premise, then the resulting conclusion is definite, and the code *always* exits. In this case, no code is needed to test for termination: RCOMPL simply inserts an unconditional exit.

(b) Otherwise, the conclusion might or might not be definite, depending on whether the premise was definite. That can only be determined at runtime, so a test for termination is inserted.

Only in case (3b) is there any runtime work to do, and this accounts for a minority of cases in practice.[12] Thus, this is another example of compile-time optimization (the rule interpreter has to test for termination *every* time a rule succeeds).

5.3.4   Self-referencing Rules

The rule interpreter requires that self-referencing rules be evaluated in a special fashion after normal rules for the same parameter are evaluated (Section 2.6.1.5). Respecting this ordering convention adds another complication to RCOMPL's task. However, the solution is fairly straightforward: RCOMPL compiles these rules in separate blocks (like rules of separate **SUBJECT**s), and lets the rule interpreter worry about evaluating them at the proper time and maintaining the pre-self-reference value. While in certain cases (viz., when all the rules for the parameter have the same **SUBJECT**) it would be possible to generate one block containing all the code for both normal and self-referencing rules, in general, separate blocks are necessary.

5.3.5   Interface to the Rule Monitor

The normal procedure followed by the monitor when tracing a parameter (Section 2.2) is to retrieve the list of rules concluding about the parameter; that list is precomputed automatically by the knowledge base maintenance routines and stored internally as the parameter's **UPDATED-BY** property.

Then for each rule in the list the monitor checks that the rule is applicable (its **SUBJECT** is suitable for the context), and finally applies the rule.

A simple modification to the procedure permits compiled rules. The **UPDATED-BY** property remains untouched, since other parts of the system use it for explanation purposes. RCOMPL instead generates an analogous property **C.UPDATED-BY**; the monitor checks this property first and, if present, uses it in preference to the original **UPDATED-BY**. The **C.UPDATED-BY** property is a list of compiled rule blocks,[13] each corresponding to one or more of the source rules in the **UPDATED-BY** list. To apply a compiled rule the monitor checks for applicability just as with interpreted rules, then executes the code of the compiled rule.

This scheme also allows intermixing of interpreted and compiled rules. The mixing is, of course, in the units of a rule block; i.e., a block of rules is either run compiled (one block of code) or wholly interpreted (as individual rules). Should the user wish to edit a rule in a compiled system,[14] the system looks up the rule in an auxiliary file to find out which compiled block it is in, and loads all the rules in that block. The edited rule and the unchanged rules in its block replace the compiled block in the **C.UPDATED-BY** list, and the consultation program can be run as usual.[15] Deleted rules are handled similarly, and new rules are simply added to the **C.UPDATED-BY** list (in interpreted form) directly. When it comes time to incorporate the changes into the system permanently, the rule file is automatically updated, and RCOMPL is called in "recompile" mode, compiling afresh only those blocks whose members have changed.

5.3.6 Interaction with the Explanation System

For general explanations, the QA module needs to examine the rule base for the rules relevant to the question being asked. In a system running compiled rules, the source rules are accessible via an external hashfile.[16] This obviously slows down the operation of rule retrieval, but since the rule base is indexed by the parameters in each part of the rules, only a portion of the rule base need be examined for any one question.

To answer questions concerning a particular consultation, the explanation subsystems currently use several records left behind by the rule interpreter. These include a history list showing when each parameter was traced (associated with the rule whose premise needed it) and each rule was invoked, a record of the conclusions made by each successful rule, and a record of the outcome of each rule tried (succeeded, or failed because of clause *n*).

The most expensive of these is recording the invocation and outcome of each rule. RCOMPL could simply compile code to leave such records, but this is undesirable. One of the principal optimizations in compiling a decision tree is that the code can totally ignore large blocks of rules that fail at once. Spending time leaving behind records for each rule that implicitly failed would be wasteful.

However, if the rule compiler can analyze the rule to determine which clauses use which parameters, the explanation system can, too, and by static evaluation figure out whether a rule is true or not. The QA module has been modified to use this strategy when the corresponding records are unavailable. Slightly less information is available by this analysis than by the explicit records, since it tells only whether (and how) the rule would fail if actually evaluated; it does not distinguish the cases of a rule that was tried and failed, a rule that was never tried because Preview pruned it as being already false, and a rule that was never even considered (either because the parameter it concluded was never traced, or was successfully concluded before the rule was tried). However, such distinctions are more useful as an aid to debugging the knowledge base than as a justification of the program's reasoning. Since one probably would not be debugging a system with compiled rules, this failure is thus not a major shortcoming.

Occasionally the QA module will not be able to determine that a rule failed (or would fail); such cases arise when the clause that fails is not symbolically evaluable (generally the same sort of clause that RCOMPL can do nothing smart with). This is a shortcoming of permitting arbitrary predicates in rules (rather than insisting on a small set of stylized and easily manipulable forms).

5.4   RCOMPL's Overall Procedure

Now that the central parts of RCOMPL have been described, Figure 5-4 shows the rough outline of the complete task: RCOMPL takes in a knowledge base, and produces a file of machine code that can be loaded in place of the rules in that knowledge base.

5.5   What the Rule Compiler Does Not Do

The algorithm described so far produces code that mimics fairly well the simple application of rules within a backward-chaining control structure. However, as flexibility is introduced into the control structure, it becomes more difficult to compile the rules to satisfy all the control options. Several operations performed by the rule interpreter involve modifying the normal control flow through a runtime examination of the rules, and thus are not

Open a file for the output code.

If recompiling, then open for input the file produced by the previous compilation.

For each parameter *P* in the knowledge base, **do**:

> Partition the rules in *P*'s UPDATED-BY list according to SUBJECT,
> separating also self-referencing from non-self-referencing rules.

> For each block *B* in the partitioned rules, **do**:

>> If *B* is unchanged since the last compilation,
>>   then copy the old code for *B* directly to the output;
>> else
>>   Scan the rules in *B* and build a table indicating which clauses
>>   in the rules imply/negate which other clauses
>>   (for use in Compile's clause selection algorithm);
>>   Apply **Compile** to *B*, producing a LISP function *B'*;
>>   Apply the common subexpression eliminator to *B'*;[17]
>>   Apply the INTERLISP compiler to *B'*, producing machine code output.

> Compute and output a C.UPDATED-BY property for *P* based on the names
> of the functions compiled above.

Close files.

Figure 5-4. The overall procedure followed by RCOMPL in transforming
the rules of a knowledge base into a file of machine-loadable code.

easily supported by RCOMPL. While for the most part the operations would not be impossible to compile, they are difficult and in most cases nonessential (to the extent described below).

5.5.1   Circular Reasoning

"Circular reasoning" occurs if the system tries to trace a parameter that is currently being traced. This is generally considered a bug in the rule set; currently the rule interpreter handles the situation more or less gracefully by aborting the rule that is attempting the circularity. The abortion is performed via an explicit stack manipulation when the value of the parameter causing the circularity is sought.[18]

Such a simple abortion procedure is not possible once the rules are compiled, since there is no discrete rule to abort. Aborting the whole block would be incorrect, since there might remain noncircular rules still untested. Logically, one wants to abort the current node in the decision tree, returning so that *neither* side of the branch is followed. However, even if one introduced the extra inefficiency of creating an explicit frame for each node in the decision tree, thus allowing the stack manipulation, the common subexpression eliminator would be weakened—subsequent computation outside of the branch could not rely on the parameter value computed at that branch, since the branch might have been bypassed.

Thus, RCOMPL currently ignores the problem of circular reasoning. This is not unreasonable, however, since one expects error recovery to be more awkward under compiled code. Since the compiler is generally not applied until a rule set is debugged, this policy should not be a problem.[19]

5.5.2 Preview

The Preview operation (Section 2.6.2.1) consists of examining a rule's clauses before actually evaluating the rule, to see if the rule is already doomed to failure. While Preview prevents some rules from being applied at all, it does not in that way necessarily save any time, since it is usually at least as difficult for the rule interpreter to determine that some clause in the rule is known to be false as it is to directly evaluate the rule. Preview's virtue is that it may avoid entirely the exploration of some subgoal tree, if the only reason for exploring it is to evaluate some clause in a rule that fails anyway.

Although RCOMPL does not produce code that explicitly Previews rules, it implicitly performs a portion of Preview's work. Whenever a branch is selected at runtime, all the rules on the false side of the branch are automatically pruned away with no explicit runtime testing (the same rules when interpreted would, in most cases, be pruned by Preview). This "implicit" Preview acts only on clauses common to the rules in one subtree of the decision tree, of course, and only after the clause has actually been evaluated once in the normal course of execution, whereas the explicit Preview performed by the rule interpreter works for clauses that have become false at *any* point in the consultation.[20] Thus, it remains a possibility that the compiled decision tree will evaluate a clause that causes tracing of a parameter that would not have been traced when the rules were interpreted. One might consider that RCOMPL is producing efficient, but slightly "dumb" code.

This shortcoming is somewhat disturbing, since it is important that a consultant not ask "too many" questions. Experience shows, however, that Preview actually performs non-trivial pruning in only a small percentage of cases.[21] A given piece of information (parameter) may be (and typically is) used in multiple rules. Thus, even if Preview avoids evaluating a clause in one rule, there may still be other rules that need the same information and will thus trace the parameter anyway.[22]

If it were deemed desirable, RCOMPL could, at some expense, explicitly compile the tests Preview makes before actually trying the rules. The obvious way would be to transform a rule

$$\textbf{if } C_1 \textbf{ and } C_2 \textbf{ and } \ldots \textbf{ and } C_n \textbf{ then } X$$

into a rule that explicitly Previews itself:

$$\begin{aligned}
(\textbf{if } \quad &(C_2 \text{ is not known } \textbf{or } C_2 \text{ is true}) \quad \textbf{and} \\
&\qquad\qquad \ldots \qquad\qquad\qquad\qquad\quad \textbf{and} \\
&(C_n \text{ is not known } \textbf{or } C_n \text{ is true}) \quad \textbf{and} \\
&\qquad C_1 \textbf{ and } C_2 \textbf{ and } \ldots \textbf{ and } C_n \\
\textbf{then } &X)
\end{aligned}$$

and then compile the transformed rule in the conventional way.[23] Even using clever coding to save the early clause evaluations (if they occur, i.e, when a clause is already known) to re-use later during the "real" evaluation of the clause, the restructured rule would itself involve a lot of redundant computation and would not be amenable to much, if any, factoring during the compilation.

A better method would be to follow the **Compile** algorithm as normal, but (1) first reorder the premises of each rule so that clauses guaranteed to be known are tried first (since these clauses never need to be protected by Preview), and (2) whenever the algorithm calls for creating a branch out of clause C_i, compile code to Preview any clause C_j, for $j < i$, that has not yet been previewed higher in the tree. This would still amount to a lot of extra code.

More desirable would be a way of reducing the incidence of unnecessary tracing without substantially increasing the runtime computational burden. The need for Preview could actually be obviated altogether if it were possible to order all parameters in such a way that for $j > i$, if parameter P_j is known, then parameter P_i is known. One could then reorder the premises of each rule to ensure that no clause could already be false when some preceding clause was not yet known. Such an order is not possible in general, since the parameters used in a consultation may vary from case to case. However, a static analysis of the rule set could produce a partial ordering; e.g., if every rule that concludes P_j uses P_i (and P_j is not an **ASKFIRST** parameter), then the relationship stated above holds. The ordering might not produce enough information to make a big dent in the Preview problem, but any reordering of clauses it implied would be guaranteed to be "correct."

A useful approximation to a total ordering might be to order the parameters by how *likely* they are to be known. For example, one might order the parameters by their frequency of use; a parameter used in only one rule might be less likely to be known than one appearing in ten.[24] The problem with this method remains, however, that the rule interpreter still expects clauses to be evaluated in the order of their appearance, and if RCOMPL changed that order, different performance might result. However, all but one of the cases noted in Section 5.6 where extra parameters were traced could have been remedied by such a reordering.

5.5.3 Unitypath

Unitypath (Section 2.6.2.2) serves a similar pruning function: if there is some rule that will make the desired conclusion with certainty, then all other rules are irrelevant (if they make any conclusions at all, even those conclusions will be overridden by the definite conclusion). Any tracing done by those unused rules is thus avoided. A second useful effect occurs if the parameter being traced is marked **ASKFIRST**; a Unitypath is sought even before asking the user, and if found avoids a question.

RCOMPL could compile a Unitypath as a separate block or blocks for each parameter (code to be invoked in place of the normal Unitypath mechanism). In the block would be any rule whose conclusion is made with certainty and whose premise might be certain. Each clause C in such a rule would be replaced by the clause "C is known and C is definitely true," and the normal compiling procedure would take place.

Whether this procedure is worth doing depends primarily on the rule set. If all rules make definite conclusions, then this would require a great deal of redundant computation; if only a few do, the compiled Unitypath is just a quick test (*much* faster than the normal Unitypath mechanism) and a small piece of code. A reasonable criterion might be "compile a Unitypath if the Unitypath block would include some but not most of the rules for the parameter, or if the parameter is marked **ASKFIRST**."

This procedure has not yet been implemented, though it is straightforward. Investigation of the local EMYCIN systems reveals that very few Unitypaths would be compiled on those systems. In MYCIN, there are a total of five parameters that would receive Unitypaths, each with only one or two rules. For PUFF there are two candidate parameters by the criterion given above, again with just one or two rules each, and further analysis reveals both of those would have no practical effect, since the rules not in the Unitypath test only parameters tested in the Unitypath. In SACON all conclusons are definite, so *every* rule for each parameter would have to be included in the parameter's Unitypath block, which would probably be excessive.

5.5.4 Metarules

Metarules reorder or prune individual object-level rules at runtime. Once a whole set of rules is compiled into one block of code, that manipulation is no longer possible. Thus, one might wish to incorporate the information in the metarules into the code produced by the rule compiler. However, metarules in their full generality are incompatible with RCOMPL. The difficulty is that metarules may juggle the runtime order of rule evaluation, or prune the list of rules being tried, on the basis of information known only at runtime. RCOMPL, however, compiles a decision tree in which the rules are tried in a fixed order, and the only pruning it can perform is the addition of extra premise clauses to the rules (to reduce the number of cases in which the rules are fully evaluated).[25]

A restricted class of metarules could be incorporated into RCOMPL: rules for which sufficient information about their effect is available at compile time. For a metarule that prunes, it is necessary that the subset of rules to be pruned can be determined from a static examination of the rules. The case-dependent clauses from the metarule can then be added as preconditions to the front of each rule in the subset to be pruned, and the rules then compiled in the normal fashion. The extra clauses introduced by the metarule would be common among all the rules in the pruned subset, and hence would be compiled efficiently as branches high in the decision tree.[26]

The constraint on a metarule that reorders the rule list is somewhat greater: the entire rule must be evaluable at compile time, since the rules can only be compiled in one, unconditional order. One type of metarule that satisfies this constraint is of the form "try rules that use parameter x before rules that use parameter y." To incorporate such a metarule into the compilation, RCOMPL would need to determine the static order implied (which might be just a partial order), and then build its sequence of decision trees in such a way as to satisfy the order. Specifically, it would obey the added constraint "never test a clause from a rule unless all rules before it in the partial ordering either (a) have been evaluated before this point, or (b) appear on the other side of the branch under which the current test falls." This would necessitate some changes to the **Compile** algorithm, since it would mean that a rule could not necessarily appear under a branch just because it contained the branch clause. The branching factor in the tree, of course, would tend to be less than that obtained without observing metarules.[27]

5.5.5 Antecedent Rules

Antecedent rules can be compiled in a fashion similar to consequent rules. In this case, the rules are grouped according to which parameters may trigger the rule. Before the rules are compiled, they are modified by adding additional premise clauses that assert that all the regular premise clauses are known (this need not be done, obviously, for the clause whose parameter triggered the rule; nor need it be done for clauses containing parameters otherwise known to be traced already). Compilation then proceeds normally. There is no premature termination to worry about, since the rules are being invoked in response to data (the parameter) just found out, rather than to make inferences about some parameter not yet known (for that matter, each of the rules may make conclusions about different parameters).

Currently, RCOMPL does not compile antecedent rules, since there are usually very few of them (due to their limited abilities), and interpreting them takes up relatively little of the consultation runtime. This practice might be changed in future implementations if the situation should change.

5.6   Timing Results

In order to determine, at least empirically, how much is saved by using the rule compiler, the knowledge bases of three EMYCIN applications were compiled. Typical consultations were then run from each system's library, and the execution times of the compiled code were compared against those of the rule interpreter handling the normal (source) rules. The timing results, shown in Figure 5-5, were broken down according to how much of the time was spent executing rules and how much was spent doing other activities, in order to isolate RCOMPL's contribution to the overall timing.

As noted above, RCOMPL does not handle Unitypath. In order that the interpreted consults not be penalized for the extra time spent trying to find Unitypaths, the Unitypath mechanism was disabled for these timing comparisons. The one parameter in the MYCIN knowledge base that uses Unitypath non-trivially was reclassified as non-**ASKFIRST** to maintain consistency.[28] The time "wasted" in Unitypath ranges from about 4% of total runtime in MYCIN and PUFF to over 15% in SACON, where the fact that all rules make definite conclusions makes Unitypath work too hard.

Only a few cases were available for testing in SACON and PUFF, so each was run twice to reduce the distortion inherent in the timing process. The 129 cases run from the MYCIN libraries consisted of 21 cases of bacteremia and 108 meningitis cases. The bacteremia cases differed from the meningitis cases in that the former typically had many more contexts and took longer (total consultation time of 175 seconds for bacteremia vs.

115 seconds for meningitis), but the percentage figures in each category were nearly identical for both sets of cases, so they are presented here together for simplicity. The average execution times for all three knowledge bases is in direct proportion to the size of their rule sets (page 33), although individual consultations with more contexts took correspondingly longer (some rules are applied more often with more contexts).[29]

Knowledge Base:	PUFF	SACON	MYCIN
1. Number of cases tested	5x2	3x2	129
2. Time spent per case in consultation with interpreted rules (cpu seconds):			
a. (consequent) Rule Interpreter	9 (55%)	26 (52%)	69 (56%)
b. Asking questions	3 (20%)	14 (28%)	22 (18%)
c. Other	4 (25%)	10 (20%)	32 (26%)
d. Total (a+b+c)	16	50	123
3. Time spent per case in consultation with compiled rules (cpu seconds):			
a. Executing compiled rules	4	7	23
b. Total consultation time	11	31	75
4. Time saved by compiled rules, expressed as a percentage of:			
a. rule interpreter time (2a)	56%	73%	67%
b. total interpreted time (2d)	31%	38%	39%
c. inter-question time (2a+2c)	39%	53%	48%

Figure 5-5. Timing comparisons of interpreted vs. compiled rules.

As the percentage figures for Item 2 indicate, these systems spend only a little over half of their execution time interpreting consequent rules, and it is with essentially only this time that RCOMPL can assist.[30] Approximately 20% is spent asking questions (principally the time required to print the prompts; I/O wait time is not included), and the remainder goes to overhead in tracing parameters, setting up contexts, and evaluating antecedent rules.[31]

The percentages in Item 4 indicate how much is saved by running compiled rules instead of interpreted. Line 4a shows how effective RCOMPL is in isolation: time spent just in evaluating rules was cut by 56% (PUFF) to 73% (SACON). Line 4b indicates how much savings results overall in the total consultation time; these figures, of course, are little over half of Line 4a, since little over half of the total time is spent in rules. However, to the interactive user, it is the time between questions that is the most important efficiency measure, since that is the system's apparent "think" time; taking this into account, Line 4c expresses the savings when the time spent in questions is ignored.

Thus, the principal result here is that RCOMPL can cut the inter-question time by close to half.

As for the claimed equivalence of compiled to interpreted rules, in all of the cases run, the program made identical conclusions for all parameters traced. Conclusions were sometimes made in a different order, however, so there were occasionally small differences (less than .005) in final CF's, due to roundoff error in the CF computation. As expected, the question order differed in some cases, mostly in MYCIN's meningitis cases, where a large number of parameters concerning the patient are asked in essentially random order.

Since RCOMPL does not take Preview into account, there were occasionally extra questions in the compiled versions. This happened in three of the five PUFF cases, in each of which the same extra question was asked, needed by the same rule. It never happened in SACON. And in the 129 MYCIN cases, it happened in seven: in six of the cases one new question was asked (corresponding to four different **ASKFIRST** parameters), but in one case the parameter that was needlessly traced was not **ASKFIRST**, and its tracing resulted in four new questions. All but one of the above cases could have been avoided by the frequency-ordering heuristic suggested in Section 5.5.2.

On the other hand, the compiled code in some cases performed pruning that was not done by Preview in the interpreted cases. In one of the MYCIN cases, the compiled code pruned a question that was needlessly asked in the interpreted case. In about one third of the MYCIN cases the compiled code avoided tracing two parameters that were traced and then not used in the interpreted case (but which did not cause any questions to be asked).[32]

5.7   Related Compiling Work

5.7.1   Pure Production Systems

The problem of inefficiency is even greater in "pure" production systems. In addition to the redundancy of repeatedly testing similar patterns in multiple rules (the problem RCOMPL concentrates on), the interpreter in conventional, non-indexed, data-driven production systems is repeatedly testing elements of working memory that have not changed, and hence will not fire rules. This is a huge waste of time if working memory is large compared to the number of memory elements that change per cycle.

Forgy describes an interpreter for OPS that "compiles" the left-hand sides of the productions [Forgy 79a]. The productions are compiled into a network of simple demons that watch changes to working memory and output the resulting changes to the conflict set. Similar left-hand sides can share nodes in the network (though there is no attempt to factor rules into mutually-exclusive sets). The network is "run" by an interpreter; Forgy also describes how one might microcode the interpreter for dramatic speedup.

Even if EMYCIN ran totally antecedent-driven, repeated testing of memory elements would be only a minor concern, since rules are indexed by parameter, and a given parameter can only trigger antecedent rules once. However, if the antecedent rules had many clauses one could imagine setting up a network of subdemons that would watch for all the parameters needed and finally fire the rule when the last parameter became known.

The LISP70 language [Tesler 73] includes as a language feature the ability to specify "rewrite rules," which are essentially data-driven rules that manipulate an input stream. The productions are compiled into efficient machine code to do the matching; the productions are factored from the left to avoid redundant computation in similar rules. The resulting code is a discrimination tree needing fewer choice points for backtracking than the original productions.

5.7.2   Decision Tables

EMYCIN rules bear some resemblance to extended-entry decision tables. Decision tables have long been used in business computing applications (see [Hughes 68] for an overview). A decision table specifies for each combination of a set of conditions to be tested (or at least some subset of combinations) what action is to be taken. A sample table is depicted in Figure 5-6.

The j conditions to be tested are listed on the left in the *condition stub*, followed by the k possible actions in the *action stub*. Each remaining column in the table corresponds to some combination of conditions, and is termed a *decision rule*. Each row in the *condition entry* portion of a rule contains the desired value of the condition (here **Y** and **N** for Yes and No), or a "−" for "don't care"; each row in the *action entry* contains an "x" for each action desired when the conditions are satisfied. A *limited-entry* decision table contains only yes/no conditions; an *extended-entry* table permits arbitrary conditions. The order of the conditions is arbitrary, and no more than one rule in a table may be satisfied at once. Some tables permit an *else* rule (often, an error condition) to be executed if none of the other rules in the table is satisfied.

condition \ rule #	1	2	3	4	· · ·	n
condition 1	Y	Y	Y	N	· · ·	—
condition 2	—	Y	—	Y	· · ·	Y
condition 3	Y	N	N	—	· · ·	N
· · ·	· ·	· ·	· ·	· ·	· · ·	· ·
condition j	N	Y	Y	—	· · ·	Y
action 1	x	x			· · ·	x
· · ·	· ·	· ·	· ·	· ·	· · ·	· ·
action k		x		x	· · ·	

Figure 5-6. A sample limited-entry decision table of *n* rules over *j* conditions. Each column of the table represents one rule. If the indicated combination of conditions is satisfied, the actions in that column checked with "x" are taken.

Decision tables are sometimes used simply as programming aids, akin to flow charts. However, there is a wealth of decision table "languages" and processors available that can convert a decision table either into running code, or into a program in an intermediate language, such as COBOL, for further processing by conventional compilers [McDaniel 70]. Those processors that convert decision tables into decision trees (programs of nested conditionals) are performing a task similar to that of RCOMPL. Procedures described in [Pollack 71] and [Montalbano 62] are quite similar to the **Compile** algorithm of this chapter. Most attention has been paid to limited-entry decision tables, as they are easier to analyze, and extended-entry tables can be converted into limited entry tables by a simple syntactic process (though with some loss of efficiency [King 65]). Fairly elaborate procedures have been described for converting limited-entry tables into decision trees optimized for time [Reinwald 66] or space [Reinwald 67].

Of course, there are significant differences between decision tables and EMYCIN rules. Decision tables do not handle uncertainty in the data or conclusions, and they do not admit multiple decision rules succeeding simultaneously (in fact, the problem of detecting such *ambiguity* in decision tables has received much attention). The order of conditions tested in a decision table is considered arbitrary; the problem of converting a decision table to a good decision tree is, in fact, one of deciding the best order to test the conditions. RCOMPL's task, on the other hand, is noticeably complicated by the restriction on order of clause evaluation.

Decision tables are also usually quite "dense" in comparison to typical EMYCIN rules, i.e., if a block of EMYCIN rules is written as a decision table, with the condition stub consisting of all conditions tested in any rule, the resulting table is typically quite sparse. Local clusters of rules may, however, resemble decision tables, including satisfying the condition that only one rule of the set may succeed in any given case (these are sets of rules for which the **while** loop in **Compile** executes only once).

The virtues of decision tables as a means of problem specification have been stated often. The decision table format might be a useful way to acquire rules in those situations where the expert is writing several rules using the same parameters, and wants to be sure to "handle every case." The expert could simply state the conditions, and then simply fill in the action as the program prompts for each combination of conditions (column in the decision table). The program would then compose rules to correspond to the decision table, or the decision table could be preserved and treated as a special kind of rule. EMYCIN already contains an Action function that behaves like a decision table with one condition.[33]

5.8 A Lesson in Language Design

RCOMPL suffers somewhat from having been an addition to an existing system, rather than a part of the original design. Had EMYCIN been designed from the outset with compilation in mind, some design decisions might have been made differently in order to simplify the task of the compiler.

The most glaring obstacle faced by RCOMPL is, perhaps, the constraint on the order of clause evaluation. In most rules, the order of evaluation of the clauses is actually irrelevant; however, the presence of the implicit ordering constraint forces RCOMPL to assume it applies to *every* rule, in some cases resulting in suboptimal code.[34] Through a certain amount of compile-time analysis, RCOMPL can determine that the order is irrelevant; it knows, for example, that it can evaluate **INITIAL-DATA** parameters in any order, and if it carried out some of the laborious static analysis suggested in Section 5.5.2 it could change the order of certain other clauses with safety. But it cannot in general determine when order is significant and when it is not. Had the rule interpreter been designed with RCOMPL in mind, it might have permitted arbitrary order of clauses, with explicit primitives to handle the cases where order matters. For example, cases where one clause now is "screened" by an earlier clause might be handled by making a global statement such as "parameter **P** is not to be traced unless condition **C** has been satisfied." Such a statement would also ease the system builder's task, as she would not have to remember to insert clause **C** in each rule that tests **P**. Another ordering primitive might simply be one that explicitly sequences the clauses in a rule, or labels the critical clauses with priority information.

Another feature of the EMYCIN design not handled well by RCOMPL is mapping rules. As they are currently written, common clauses cannot be conveniently factored from such rules. Mapping rules have other shortcomings as well, and the remedy suggested in Section 6.1.2 to make mapping rules easier to write and understand would probably aid in their compilation as well.

6

Conclusions

6.1 Assumptions and Limitations

EMYCIN was not designed to be a general-purpose representation language. It is thus wholly unsuited for some problems. Even those domains that have been successfully implemented have demonstrated some of the inadequacies of EMYCIN. The discussion that follows explores some of the limitations of EMYCIN and the assumptions that it makes about its domain and users (expert and client).

6.1.1 The Nature of the Task

EMYCIN is designed to handle tasks that can be posed in the form of providing consultative advice. The system takes as input a body of measurements or other information pertinent to a case, and produces as output some form of recommendation or analysis of the case. The framework seems well suited for some deductive problems, notably some classes of fault diagnosis, where a large body of input measurements (symptoms, laboratory tests) is available and the solution space of possible diagnoses can be enumerated. It is less well suited for "formation" problems, where the task is to piece together existing structures according to specified constraints to generate a solution. Among other classes of problems that EMYCIN does not attempt to handle are simulation tasks and tasks involving planning with stepwise refinement.

These limitations derive largely from the fact that EMYCIN has chosen one basic, readily understood representation for the knowledge in a domain: production rules applied by a backward-chaining control structure and operating on data in the form of associative triples. There are two principal components of that representational choice: the static representation (rules and triples) and the control structure that manipulates that representation to perform reasoning in the domain. The implications each of these has for the applicability of EMYCIN to a particular domain are discussed in the following sections.

6.1.2   *Triples*

While both production rules and associative triples are in a sense general representations, they are not necessarily natural for every problem. In some domains they may work only if the knowledge is "unnaturally" coerced into that form.[1] Generally this is undesirable—if the representation is awkward for the problem, it will be difficult to build a whole knowledge base, and some of the benefits of the EMYCIN representation, such as explanation ability, may be lost. Thus, the extent to which such coercion is necessary may dictate whether the use of EMYCIN is feasible. It may be acceptable to use a suboptimal representation for a problem if the goal is to quickly test out some rules for the problem, rather than to build an extensive system.

The representation of facts as associative triples (with CF's) has proved a flexible enough data structure in our investigations thus far. Many simple facts have the nature of triples—an attribute of an object is some value—an observation attested to by the popularity of property lists in LISP-like languages and the many frame-oriented representation languages. However, triples are not an effective or natural representation for some tasks. For example, although it was possible to write graph matching rules in DENDRAL in terms of triples [Buchanan 69], they were found to be quite cumbersome; the more compact representation of connection tables for chemical graphs was found to be much more effective.

In addition, EMYCIN places further assumptions on the nature of the triples by the way in which rules are permitted to manipulate them. Triples are not symmetric; they work best in EMYCIN when the objects (contexts) are well-organized and few in number, at least as compared to the number of attributes (parameters). The principal reason for this is the limited manner in which rules may refer to contexts. Rules are easiest to understand when they make no explicit mention of contexts. Note, for example, that ARL expressions do not involve contexts, only parameters and their values. That arrangement works well when a rule refers only to parameters of contexts that lie along the same path to the root of the context tree, since then the extra contexts involved are implicitly the ancestors of the context to which the rule is applied. However, when a rule needs to refer to parameters of contexts that are not so simply related in the context tree, the rule must make explicit mention of the additional context(s) it uses and the manner in which they are to be used. Such rules tend to be awkward both to write and to understand (for example, see

Rule 182 on page 30, or the section describing mapping rules in Appendix A). Thus, triples are most easily manipulated in domains where the objects form a natural, fixed hierarchy and where the rules do not often speak of facts from divergent branches of the hierarchy.

This restriction on the use of contexts could be substantially remedied in EMYCIN by providing more powerful mechanisms for instantiating contexts and forming links between them. Currently, only links corresponding to the static hierarchy of context types are "built in" to the rule language; other links can be made, but not conveniently. As noted in Section 2.6.3.3, when the contexts are not already directly linked in the context tree, mapping rules have to be written. Even though they may be performing the same sort of inference as ordinary rules, mapping rules tend to be much more difficult to comprehend, as they require too much explicit statement of what the iteration set is, and it is hard to express bindings in English. This also reflects the problem of control knowledge in rules that were not designed to accommodate it (see Section 6.1.3 below). The need for many explicit mapping rules could be removed by allowing a rule to specify, as a separate component, what type of additional contexts the rule can be applied to (in addition to the original context of the rule). Such a component in a MYCIN rule might say, for example, "this rule applies to positive cultures and any infections that have been determined [by other rules] to be associated with the culture."

A further restriction on triples is that it is difficult to represent any values except simple values, whereas in real problems there is often an extra dimension involved: the *attribute* of *object* at *variable* is *value*. A common extra variable is time. For example, a patient's temperature is not a single value, but is a function of time; signal interpretation tasks (e.g., speech understanding) typically work with large arrays of time-dependent data. EMYCIN, however, is currently oriented toward reasoning about a single, static snapshot of a case, with no convenient means of reasoning about case data changing over time[2] or examining trends in time-related data (e.g., a *rising* temperature).[3] One way to represent time-dependent values within the existing framework of triples is to introduce a new context type, say "the state of the patient." One parameter of the context would be the time represented by an instance of the context, and the remaining parameters would have values associated with that particular time.[4] However, as noted above, the introduction of new contexts may simply lead to more awkward rules. One would need convenient ways to select the state context that was relevant to the other information being tested in the rule, and predicates that could compare states less awkwardly than EMYCIN's current mapping rules.

6.1.3 Rules

The concept of production rules is also quite general—Post's productions are, after all, equivalent to a Turing machine. EMYCIN maintains that generality by permitting arbitrary LISP expressions in rules. However, it in some sense only supports a standard set of predicates and conclusion functions, in that the system features that are able to reason about the form of rules often only "know" the semantics of some of the built-in predicates. In some cases it suffices that a new predicate have a template with certain recognized tokens, to allow the system to pick out, for example, the parameter referenced in a given clause. In other cases, more specific knowledge of the behavior of the predicate is needed; e.g., Preview needs to know when it can safely evaluate a clause without side effect (viz., the tracing of a parameter), and Unitypath needs to know under what circumstances a clause will return a value with certainty.

With rules as the primary form of representing relations among fact triples, it is inevitable that not all forms of knowledge are equally well expressed. EMYCIN rules appear suitable for direct statements of judgmental knowledge, but serve less well to embody strategical or control knowledge.[5] In all of the EMYCIN knowledge bases to date there have been some rules that exist solely to affect the control structure explicitly (e.g., trace parameters in a certain order). Rules of this sort do not always appear to "make sense," especially when compared directly to judgmental rules. Other systems have tried to handle this by explicitly separating out the control knowledge, either into separate rules or into a wholly different data structure, and manipulating the two independently. For example, CENTAUR uses frames to impose structure and explicit control knowledge on the rules of an EMYCIN domain [Aikins 80].

There can also be a problem in maintaining a knowledge base when it grows very large. EMYCIN does not provide any global structure for the rules, other than to index them (automatically) by the parameters they use or conclude, and to classify them by context. While rules are stated as small, modular packets of knowledge, closely related rules cannot necessarily be considered in isolation for purposes of either explanation or knowledge acquisition. Often a set of several rules is written to cover several subcases of one general "setting," each rule containing the same small set of initial clauses to establish that setting, and further clauses to distinguish the subcase. It is not apparent from examination of one such rule that it is part of such a larger set of rules, and that the particular clauses tested or the certainty assigned to the conclusion were written on the assumption that other rules in the set are handling related cases not covered by this rule.

While this lack of explicit organization does not inherently limit the use of rules as a representation, it would be desirable to have a means of organizing and using such information to aid in maintaining the knowledge base and providing higher-level explanations to a user. It would be possible to write routines for EMYCIN that aided the knowledge acquisition process by automatically organizing the rules by content, locating rules related to a given one, and finding gaps in the knowledge base. But it would also be desirable to allow the expert to choose classifications directly meaningful to those familiar with the domain, e.g., "rules for viral meningitis."[6]

The fact that rules are expected to be judgmental suggests that the knowledge of some domains may not be effectively represented in rules. Some of the simpler knowledge bases (PUFF, SACON) make little or no use of the inexact inference mechanism provided by CF's. More efficient representations may exist for the precise knowledge existing in such domains; e.g., much of the SACON rule set might be more concisely and lucidly represented as decision tables. However, even in such cases it is still practical to build a reasoning program from EMYCIN as a first test of the inference rules written by an expert. While many of the system's complicated features, such as certainty factors and the context tree, may go unused in the simpler systems, those features do not substantially burden a program that does not use their extra generality.

6.1.4 Control Structure

The goal-directed, depth-first, backward-chaining control structure EMYCIN uses to apply the rules is perhaps the greatest limitation on the nature of the task an EMYCIN consultant can handle. Backward chaining works well for simple deductive tasks, but as soon as a problem poses additional constraints on the means by which reasoning can or should be performed, more sophisticated control mechanisms may be required. Some additional control information can be embodied in rules, through such means as ordering the clauses of critical rules, but this is starting to stretch the capabilities of EMYCIN rules, and can result in the loss of some of their benefits. Antecedent rules and metarules can also exert a certain amount of control influence, but their use is still confined to local changes within the overall backward-chaining structure.

Backward chaining is certainly inadequate as a general control structure for many problems. The discussion that follows, however, concentrates principally on shortcomings of EMYCIN's control structure that have been noted in actual EMYCIN applications and in related problems.

Constraint satisfaction.   EMYCIN provides no general means of achieving goals in the presence of multiple constraints; any sophisticated optimization technique needs to be hand-coded. For example, the process of therapy selection in MYCIN is such a problem: backward-chained rules cannot adequately express the simultaneous goals of minimizing the number of drugs prescribed while maximizing their coverage. To perform therapy selection, then, MYCIN has a specially customized procedure using a generate and test paradigm that is invoked in the action of a rule. The generator is very specific to the problem, generating potential therapies in a best-first order; rules are used to perform further testing before accepting a therapy thus generated.

Iterative solution techniques.   EMYCIN is oriented toward solving a very "static" problem. Every parameter is either known or not, but its value never changes once known. There is thus no way to make an approximate guess, then refine it in successive passes, finally converging on the correct solution, beyond the quite limited means of using self-referencing rules.

Focus of reasoning.   On a slightly more general level, backward chaining assumes that there is a "direct path" from the input data to the final output. Reasoning is then a simple matter of cranking through all the relevant rules and propagating conclusions. The current goal may be suspended in order to work on a subgoal (trace a parameter needed in the current rule), but the suspension of goals obeys a strict stack discipline— once the subgoal is achieved, reasoning may continue on the current goal. It is never the case that the order in which subgoals are selected is critical—the system can work on any subgoal and not be blocked. The control structure provides no way to dynamically choose one subproblem on which to focus the reasoning effort, and then suspend it until more information becomes available from another part of the problem. For example, although one could write general production rules to express the individual situation-action transformations involved in solving a cryptarithmetic problem, it would be difficult to apply them using EMYCIN's control structure—there is no way to express the strategy of focusing on arbitrary subparts of the problem, selecting only those parts for which enough is known to solve them right now, and backtracking to solve cases with a limited set of alternatives.

Focus of dialogue.   EMYCIN provides few explicit means of controlling the order in which the dialogue proceeds. The context tree, together with

INITIALDATA and **GOALS** parameters does impose a certain amount of structure on the order of questions, and the order of the clauses in any one rule dictates the relative order in which any questions generated by those clauses are asked.[7] Beyond that, however, questions are asked in the order in which the rules require the information. The tabular input mechanism attempts to overcome this to some extent by asking related questions together, but may not be suitable in cases for which it is not known whether all of the parameters asked in one table will actually be needed. Metarules can affect the order in which rules are tried, and hence indirectly have some effect on the order of questions, but such constraints are not always easy or possible to state via metarules (e.g., the constraint "always ask x before y" cannot be stated explicitly).[8]

Amount of information requested.   A major problem for computer consultants, and to some extent for human consultants as well, is controlling the amount of information requested from the client. In a long consultation, the sheer volume of information that the client is required to supply for the program's reasoning can be burdensome, thereby hindering acceptance of the program. Ideally, the consultant should only ask questions that are *really* necessary, considering the costs and benefits of each question—the cost of obtaining the information (e.g., a risky lab test) or simply the cost of bothering the client with another question, compared with the benefit in terms of how much the information will help in determining the correct solution.

While EMYCIN has a reason for each question it asks (viz., the parameter is **INITIALDATA** or is needed by a rule currently under consideration), it treats all questions equally, and makes no analysis of what eventual use will be made of the information.[9] For the medical domain of MYCIN it was considered important that the program follow the cautious strategy of considering *all* possibilities in its reasoning, even obscure ones. However, the procedure of trying all the rules relevant to the current goal, unless terminated prematurely due to a definite conclusion being made, can result in asking questions even beyond the point where the information acquired can have any significant effect on the final conclusion.

Some systems handle this better. For example, PROSPECTOR [Duda 78] selects questions to ask by examining the rules relevant to the current model and determining what piece of data will contribute the most information to the current goal. If no question would make a significant contribution, none is asked. A portion of this strategy could be used to improve EMYCIN's current control structure even within the framework of depth-first backward chaining.[10]

A related problem occurs with large knowledge bases where the hypothesis space is large. Without any explicit focus of control, a simple backward-chaining system will tend to explore all the hypotheses if there is any information to remotely suggest any of them, even if only a small number of hypotheses is strongly implicated by the case data. This problem is not strictly confined to backward chaining; its difficulty has been reviewed by Pople [Pople 77].

Another part of the problem may be due to the fact that EMYCIN does not accept volunteered information.[11] Volunteering the major facts of the case at the outset might not save the client any typing, but could save some of the overhead of printing all the individual questions, and the aggravation to the client of having to enter all the information one piece at a time in the order in which the system chooses to ask it. A more dramatic improvement could be realized if EMYCIN were connected to an on-line database containing information about the cases for which the client is seeking advice; the client would only have to answer the questions for which the database could not supply an answer.

6.1.5   Assumptions about the Expert

EMYCIN makes some assumptions about the skill of the expert and/or system designer. For best results, the system designer needs to be familiar with the LISP environment in which EMYCIN resides. Although we have substantially reduced the dependence on LISP from earlier versions, EMYCIN makes use of LISP's structure-based editor;[12] more complex rules, such as mapping rules, must be expressed in LISP forms; any new predicates needed for a domain must be programmed in LISP by the designer; and some system utilities are accessible only through interaction with LISP.[13] The designer must also be comfortable with the ideas of rules, facts triples, and backward chaining.

We have no examples yet of computer-naive experts successfully building a knowledge base without an intermediary. This is not so much due to any reliance on LISP, since simple knowledge bases at least can be constructed without any direct reference to it (cf. Chapter 3), as it is a problem of translation of the expert's knowledge into rule form. EMYCIN, as is the case with most other knowledge representation systems, assumes that the expert is able to express the domain knowledge *somehow* in the chosen representation. Although ARL assists with the final stage of this translation, providing a more convenient form in which to state a rule than the ultimate LISP form, EMYCIN does not aid in the more difficult phase of converting the expert's judgmental knowledge into the precise representation of production rules. This phase may make up a substantial part of the initial effort in producing a rule-based consultant.

Formulating the domain knowledge into production rules (or any other representation) is not an easy task. The expert must make explicit statements of the problem to be solved, the goals of the consultation, the important concepts of the domain; and finally, the rules themselves. In our experience, the model for this process has been that a person ("knowledge engineer") familiar with EMYCIN's representation interacts with the expert, elucidating the task to be performed and the particular knowledge needed for reasoning in the domain. After obtaining the outline of the knowledge base to be constructed, the knowledge engineer and expert jointly construct an initial knowledge base in EMYCIN. A process of debugging and further refinement of the expert's initial structures then follows, until the knowledge base is sufficiently complete.

6.1.6   *Assumptions about the Client*

EMYCIN makes few assumptions about the skill of the client. The consultation program produced by the system designer can be tailored to suit the expected expertise of the general class of clients. For example, if the client is expected to be sophisticated, prompts for information during the consultation can be written more tersely. For a more naive clientele the designer may write rules to conclude some piece of judgmental data that could be asked directly of a sophisticated user. In any case, the designer chooses the vocabulary, prompts, and rules that the intended clients can understand.

EMYCIN does not provide, however, any explicit "client profile" mechanism to allow the designer to write *one* knowledge base to accommodate clients of different skill levels.[14] The designer should construct the knowledge base with the "average" client in mind. Around this average, EMYCIN can accommodate some minor variation in skill. For clients less skilled than the average, the designer may specify "reprompts" that elaborate on the original question when the client types "?" in confusion; for more skilled clients, the consultation program can be run in a "terse" mode, in which some questions are phrased more tersely than the standard questions.[15]

There is a limit to how naive a client may be for which the designer can provide. The explanation program, for example, assumes that the client is able to understand the rules of the domain as an explanation of the program's reasoning. That level of explanation is inappropriate for a client unfamiliar with the concepts of the domain.

6.1.7   Size of the Problem

The difficulties of focus of control and restraining the amount of information requested during a consultation may limit the size of the problem that can be handled within the EMYCIN representational framework. We have no good measure of the complexity of domains for which these difficulties become overwhelming, as most of the applications to date have been small, prototypical systems.

However, a more immediate constraint on the size of the problem is imposed by the address space limitations in the current EMYCIN implementation. A very rough measure of the size of the problem is the number of rules and parameters in the knowledge base. The largest knowledge base (MYCIN) is definitely straining the existing limits. It contains 450 rules and nearly 200 parameters, with much additional domain-specific code (therapy selection, additional predicates) and static tables. A knowledge base consisting of just rules and parameters, and that confined itself largely to existing EMYCIN predicates, could probably grow as much as 20% large than that.[16] The other knowledge bases are no more than half that size, and well within the limits.

Facilities exist for the larger knowledge bases to store some less frequently used parts of the parameter information and auxiliary static structures on secondary storage, reading them into main memory only as needed.[17] It is also possible to "swap" rules, but this is less effective, since even though only a small subset of the rule base may actually succeed in a particular consultation, the rule interpreter usually has to examine most or all of the rules for every parameter that is traced. A knowledge base might partition well into rules for different types of cases, but EMYCIN has no high-level switching mechanism to select just the rules needed based on a few pieces of case data. Using the rule compiler in the present implementation *does* provide a space gain, however, as INTERLISP-10 automatically swaps compiled code. Thus a knowledge base that was short on space during its development could still produce an effective consultation program once the rules were compiled.

6.2   Advantages of EMYCIN

Despite the limitations, there are advantages to using EMYCIN. The environment that EMYCIN provides the system designer is tailored to rapid construction of a consultation program. Although the representational choices in EMYCIN are limited, they do support inexact reasoning and the incorporation of a certain amount of strategical information. For problems that fit the structure, high performance in the resulting consultation program is possible.

6.2.1 Design Aids

The many features of the system-building environment described in Chapter 4 greatly simplify the task of the system designer. A convenient language (ARL) is provided in which to express and read the rules of the domain, and mechanisms that automatically detect most simple input errors help ensure that the rules are stated correctly. Other bookkeeping mechanisms relieve the designer of some of the burden of system maintenance.

EMYCIN's human-engineering features, in addition to providing a pleasing environment for the system designer, simplify the task of producing a consultation program that the client can feel comfortable using. The designer has control over the way in which questions are phrased, and can provide additional information via help mechanisms to accommodate some variation in the level of skill of the clients.

EMYCIN provides several facilities to aid the designer in debugging and maintaining the knowledge base. These range from the active assistance of a TEIRESIAS-like debugger that methodically searches a faulty inference chain to locate errors, to more passive mechanisms (the explanation program, rule interpreter debugging printout) that grant the initiative to the designer. The case library facilities and Batch program make it easy to test additions to a knowledge base on old cases known to be handled correctly, automatically detecting situations where corrections to the knowledge base to handle one case result in degrading its performance on other cases.

The effect of all these design aids is that an expert can use EMYCIN to rapidly build the initial version of a rule-based consultant. It is therefore possible to determine quickly whether any particular formulation of the expert's knowledge into rules is reasonable and warrants a more extended effort, or whether a particular problem is even suitable for this representation. For a problem of small to medium size whose feasibility has been determined, EMYCIN permits the construction of an efficient, effective consultation program in a much shorter time than it could be constructed from scratch.

6.2.2 Representation

Although EMYCIN's representation is limited in scope, it does support the reasoning needed for a class of problems. The mechanism of certainty factors permits inexact reasoning, using judgmental rules operating on uncertain data. The system can reason in the absence of complete knowledge of a case, as rules can be written to utilize many alternative pieces of information to arrive at a conclusion (the strength of which reflects the knowledge behind it).

It should be noted that the use of a simple, constrained representation enables some of EMYCIN's features: the rules can be used for explanation, since the framework in which they are applied is easily understood; the debugger can mimic the backward-chaining control structure to guide the debugging process; the rules can be readily compiled into an efficient form for execution; the knowledge acquisition routines can provide guidance and error detection because the language of rules is so strongly "typed." Another advantage to the simple framework is that during the initial formulation of the domain knowledge, the simple representation and control structure allow the expert to focus on the knowledge in the rules themselves, and not be sidetracked by a bewildering array of representation or control choices.

6.2.3   Summary

We have thus seen that EMYCIN provides an effective domain-independent framework for constructing rule-based consultation programs. The consultation program produced by an expert is comfortable for a client to use, and is able to provide explanations of its reasoning by examination of its own knowledge base. For problem areas that fit the representation, the consultation program produced by the expert using EMYCIN is capable of high performance, as demonstrated at least by the diagnostic portion of the MYCIN program [Yu 79a]. The system provides an environment that is conducive to building expert knowledge bases quickly, featuring a convenient language for rules, extensive error checking and guidance during knowledge acquisition, and other human-engineering features to make the job go smoother. And through the use of the rule compiler, the system designer can ensure a degree of efficiency in the consultant's performance.

Appendix A

Catalogue of Rule Functions

Every rule has a *premise* and an *action*. The premise is of the form

($AND *clause*₁ *clause*₂ . . . *clause*ₙ).

When a rule is applied, each of the clauses is evaluated, in the order stated. The premise is true if each of the clauses is "true"; if any clause is false, evaluation stops immediately. A clause is "true" if its value is a CF that exceeds the "true" threshold (.2). For convenience in using LISP predicates or other functions whose value is not a CF, the value **NIL** (false) is treated as CF = 0, and any other value (true) is treated as CF = 1.0. The CF of the entire premise, i.e., the value of the $AND, is the minimum of the CF's of any of its clauses. This certainty is available to the action as the value of the variable **TALLY**.

The *action* of a rule is either a single conclusion, or, if there are multiple conclusions, a form

(**DO-ALL** *conclusion*₁ *conclusion*₂ . . . *conclusion*ₙ).

If the premise of the rule is true, then the action is evaluated. Each "conclusion" may actually be an arbitrary action, but usually is a simple conclusion of the value of a parameter of a context.

For expressions in both the premise and action, "evaluation" is similar to that in LISP, but EMYCIN uses a slightly different quoting convention for convenience, since rules usually deal in constants, rather than variables. Stated briefly, the convention is that atoms are left unevaluated unless they are explicitly labeled as variables.[1]

The sections that follow describe the functions supplied in EMYCIN, grouped in the following categories:

Simple predicates—functions that make up the clauses in a premise.
Conclusion functions—functions called in the action.
Auxiliary functions—functions that may be used for computing values in a premise or action.
Functions for mapping rules—functions and predicates that allow a rule to perform some operation on a whole set of contexts or values, not restricted to the normal relationships in the context tree.

The discussion is solely in terms of LISP expressions. The most common functions can be conveniently entered in ARL; see Appendix B for details.

In the descriptions that follow, the argument *cntxt* is always filled by a context variable, usually **CNTXT** (the context to which the rule is applied), but for mapping rules it may be filled by specified mapping variables. The argument *parm* is always filled by the name of a parameter.

A.1   Simple Predicates

Each clause in a rule's premise is a call to one of the predicates in the system. Predicates perform some test on the fact triples and either return true or false, or return a CF indicating the certainty with which the clause is true.

A.1.1   Non-Numeric Predicates

Matching against specific values: **SAME**[*cntxt, parm, valu*], *et al.*   The following nine functions match the value of *parm* of *cntxt* against a specified value or set of values, and return true, false, or a CF, depending on the outcome of the match. The argument *valu* is filled by a single value of the parameter, or by a form that evaluates to a value, a simple list of values, or a list of (value, cf) pairs (usually the result of the function **VAL** (q.v.)). For yes/no parameters, *valu* is omitted (**YES** is assumed). The certainty of the match between *valu* and the value of the parameter is determined as follows:

(a) if *valu* is a single value (the most common case), then the certainty of the match is just the certainty associated with the triple (*cntxt, parm, valu*) if it exists, or zero if it is unknown;

(b) If *valu* is a simple list of values, then the certainty is the maximum CF obtained by matching each value individually;

(c) If *valu* is a list of (value, cf) pairs (an unusual case), then the certainty is the maximum CF obtained by matching the individual pairs, where each individual match also takes into account the CF's of the matching values.[2]

The nine predicates each test the certainty resulting from the match and return "true" if it falls in the correct range. The predicates **SAME** and **THOUGHTNOT** are the only ones that return CF's; all others return simply true or false (1.0 or 0). **SAME** returns the result of the match unaltered; **THOUGHTNOT** returns the negation of the CF. The behavior of the predicates can best be visualized by observing the ranges on the "CF number line" shown below.

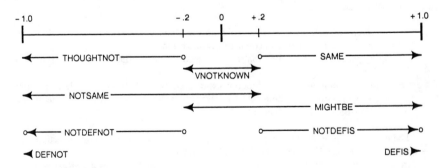

Examples of the predicates are shown below. In these and subsequent examples in this appendix, each LISP example is followed by EMYCIN's translation of the expression, with boldface used to highlight portions of the translation that relate specifically to the function being illustrated. Most of the examples are taken from the MYCIN knowledge base. **SAME** and **NOTSAME** (which are negations of each other) are by far the most commonly used of these predicates.

SAME   [true if $.2 < \text{CF} \le 1.0$]
               (SAME CNTXT SITE BLOOD)
               *The site of the culture **is** blood.*

NOTSAME   [true if $-1.0 \le \text{CF} \le .2$]
               (NOTSAME CNTXT SPECSTAIN)
               *Organisms **were not** seen on the stain of the culture.*

MIGHTBE   [true if $-.2 \le \text{CF} \le 1.0$]
               (MIGHTBE CNTXT ADEQUATE)
               *There **is no evidence that** the dose of the drug **was not** appropriate.*

THOUGHTNOT [true if $-1.0 \le \text{CF} < -.2$]
               (THOUGHTNOT CNTXT IDENT E.COLI)
               *There **is evidence that** the identity of the organism **is not** E.coli.*

VNOTKNOWN [true if $-.2 \le \text{CF} \le .2$]
               (VNOTKNOWN CNTXT IDENT E.COLI)
               *It **is not known whether** the identity of the organism is E.coli.*

DEFIS   [true if $\text{CF} = 1.0$]
               (DEFIS CNTXT IDENT MYCOBACTERIUM-TB)
               *It **is definite that** the identity of the organism **is** Mycobacterium-tb.*

DEFNOT   [true if $\text{CF} = -1.0$]
               (DEFNOT CNTXT IDENT VIRUS)
               *It **is definite that** the identity of the organism **is not** Virus.*

NOTDEFIS   [true if $.2 < \text{CF} < 1.0$]
               (NOTDEFIS CNTXT IDENT CRYPTOCOCCUS)
               *It **is suspected that** the identity of the organism **is** Cryptococcus.*

NOTDEFNOT [true if $-1.0 < \text{CF} < -.2$]
               (NOTDEFNOT CNTXT IDENT E.COLI)
               *It **is suspected that** the identity of the organism **is not** E.coli.*

Value-independent predicates: KNOWN[*cntxt, parm* **], et al.**

The following four predicates test how certain the system is of the value of *parm* of *cntxt*, independent of what the value actually is. Each predicate tests the CF associated with the most highly-confirmed value of the parameter; for yes/no parameters, it tests the absolute value of the CF.

DEFINITE   [true if CF = 1.0]
        (DEFINITE CNTXT IDENT)
        The identity of the organism is known with certainty.

KNOWN   [true if CF > .2]
        (KNOWN CNTXT IDENT)
        *The identity of the organism is **known**.*

NOTDEFINITE   [true if CF ≠ 1.0]
        (NOTDEFINITE CNTXT IDENT)
        *The identity of the organism is **not known with certainty**.*

NOTKNOWN   [true if CF ≤ .2]
        (NOTKNOWN CNTXT IDENT)
        *The identity of the organism is **not known**.*

Logic

$AND[*clause1, clause2, ... , clauseN*]
        True if *all* of the clauses are true. The CF returned is the minimum CF returned by any clau
        The clauses are evaluated in order, and evaluation stops if one fails. This function is found
        the top level of every rule premise.

$OR[*clause1, clause2, ... , clauseN*]
        True if *any* of the clauses are true. The CF returned is the maximum CF returned by any clau
        The clauses are evaluated in order, and evaluation stops if one of the clauses returns a CF
        1.0.

$NOT[*clause*]
        True if *clause* is false, false if *clause* is true. The value of the $NOT is strictly true or false, b
        clause may be a form that returns a CF.

Control predicates

ONCEKNOWN[*cntxt, parm*]
        Finds the value of *parm* of *cntxt*, but returns true regardless of whether any value was fou
        for it. Thus, the role of this "predicate" is to ensure that *parm* of *cntxt* is traced.

        (ONCEKNOWN CNTXT SAMEBUG)
        ***An attempt has been made to deduce** the organisms with possibly the same identity as
        the organism.*

ONCEKNOWN*[*cntxt, parms*]
        Traces each of the parameters in the list *parms*, i.e., like multiple calls to ONCEKNOWN.

        (ONCEKNOWN* CNTXT '(CURTHER PRIORTHER))
        ***Information has been gathered about** current drugs of the patient **and** prior drugs of
        the patient.*

A.1.2 Numeric Predicate Functions

EMYCIN supplies five numeric predicates for use with parameters that take on numeric values. The arguments to each predicate listed here are numbers or numeric expressions involving the values of numeric parameters, standardly accessed by the function **VAL1** (see **Auxiliary Functions**). Numeric expressions may use the LISP functions **PLUS, DIFFER-ENCE, MINUS, TIMES, FQUOTIENT, FIX,** and **EXPT**. For convenience, if any argument to a numeric predicate or numeric function is **NIL** (as happens when a parameter is unknown), the entire expression's value is taken to be **NIL**. When translated, the numeric predicates include the units, if any, of the parameter being compared, and may perform unit conversion to improve readability. For example:

(BETWEEN* (VAL1 CNTXT AGE) .25 10)
The age of the patient is between 3 months and 10 years.

The predicates are as follows:

BETWEEN*[*valu, llim, ulim*]	true if *llim* $\leq$ *valu* < *ulim*
GREATEQ*[*x, y*]	true if $x \geq y$
GREATERP*[*x, y*]	true if $x > y$
LESSEQ*[*x, y*]	true if $x \leq y$
LESSP*[*x, y*]	true if $x < y$

A.2 Conclusion Functions

Arbitrary LISP expressions may appear in the *action* of a rule, but usually each clause in the action concludes about one or more fact triples. The strength of each conclusion may be indicated by a CF in the conclusion clause, and will be furthered modified by the certainty of the premise of the rule (passed as the variable **TALLY**) at the time the rule is applied.[3] If the triple already exists (by a previous conclusion), its old CF is "combined" with the new CF; otherwise, a new triple is created with the new CF as its certainty.

In the following functions, the argument *tally* is always filled with the atom **TALLY**. The argument *cf* is filled with the desired certainty factor (usually a number, though it is also possible to have a form that evaluates to a CF), with a negative CF to indicate a negative conclusion; the CF's are represented as integers in the range [–1000, 1000].

Some more elaborate conclusion functions are listed under **Mapping Functions**.

CONCLUDE[*cntxt, parm, valu, tally, cf*]
Concludes that *parm* of *cntxt* is *valu*. *Valu* is a simple value of *parm* or (rarely) a computed form. If *parm* is a yes/no parameter, *valu* is YES for a positive conclusion, NO for a negative conclusion (or YES with a negative CF).

(CONCLUDE CNTXT IDENT E.COLI TALLY 400)
There is weakly suggestive evidence (.4) that the identity of the organism is E.Coli.

(CONCLUDE CNTXT CONTAMINANT NO TALLY 800) *or*
(CONCLUDE CNTXT CONTAMINANT YES TALLY -800)
There is strongly suggestive evidence (.8) that the organism is not a contaminant.

CONCLUDETEXT[*cntxt, parm, valu, tally, cf*]
This function is the same as **CONCLUDE**, except that *valu* is a "text" value, i.e., an arbitrary string of text for the text-valued parameter *parm*. Commonly, *valu* is a call to the function **TEXT** (see **Auxiliary functions**). The major difference between the two functions is in the translation.

```
(CONCLUDETEXT CNTXT FINDINGS_OAD (TEXT $OVERINFL) TALLY 1000)
```
It is definite (1.0) that the following is one of the findings about the diagnosis of obstructive airways disease: Elevated lung volumes indicate overinflation.

CONCLUDE*[*cntxt, parm, tally, valus*]
Performs multiple **CONCLUDE**'s for a single *cntxt* and *parm*. *Valus* is a quoted list of pairs (*value cf*); each value is concluded with the corresponding CF.

```
(CONCLUDE* CNTXT IDENT TALLY '((E.COLI 400)
                             (KLEBSIELLA-PNEUMONIAE 300)))
```
There is evidence that the identity of the organism is E.coli (.4) Klebsiella-pneumoniae (.3).

CONCLUDET[*cntxt, switchnum, cases, tally, parm, valus*]
This is a "tabular" conclusion function: a decision table of one condition. It concludes that *parm* of *cntxt* is one or more of the values in *valus* depending on the value of the condition *switchnum*, a numeric expression (most commonly a call to **VAL1** for a numeric parameter). *Valus* is a quoted list of simple values for *parm*. *Cases* is a quoted list of mutually-exclusive cases, each of which indicates a range for *switchnum* and a list of CF's with which to conclude each of the *valus* when *switchnum* is in the indicated range. The possible cases are as follows:

(**LT** *num* cf_1 cf_2 ... cf_n) — succeeds when *switchnum* < *num*.
(**GE** *num* cf_1 cf_2 ... cf_n) — succeeds when *switchnum* $\geq$ *num*.
(**BT** *llim ulim* cf_1 cf_2 ... cf_n) — succeeds when *llim* $\leq$ *switchnum* < *num*.
(**U** cf_1 cf_2 ... cf_n) — "Unknown": succeeds when *switchnum* = **NIL**.

Each cf_i corresponds to a $value_i$ in *valus*. If a particular value is not concluded in a case, its cf is zero.

```
(CONCLUDET CNTXT (VAL1 CNTXT LENSIGN)
           '((LT 13 -400 -500)
             (BT 13 20 -500 -400)
             (GE 20 600 300))
           TALLY TYPE '(BACTERIAL VIRAL))
```
The type of the infection is as follows:
If the duration of the neurological signs is:
a) less than 13 days then: not bacterial (.4), not viral (.5);
b) between 13 days and 20 days then: not bacterial (.5), not viral (.4);
c) greater or equal to 20 days then: bacterial (.6), viral (.3).

The following "conclusion" functions represent control knowledge.

DONTASK[*cntxt, parm*]
Indicates that *parm* of *cntxt* should never be asked, although it may be traced if needed.

```
(DONTASK CNTXT CONFORM)
```
Don't ask about the growth conformation of the organism.

NOTRELEVANT[*cntxt, parms*]
    Indicates that the value of each of the parameters in *parms* is not relevant for *cntxt*: none of the parameters should be traced (asked or deduced).

```
(NOTRELEVANT CNTXT '(MORPH FORM AIRGROW))
```
    The following are irrelevant: the morphology of the organism, the shape of the individual organisms and whether the organism was able to grow aerobically.

PRINTCONCLUSIONS[*cntxt, parm, header, evenifnil*]
    This is a simple conclusions printer that can be used to display the "results" (or intermediate conclusions) of the consultation at a time of the designer's choosing. It displays nicely the value of *parm* of *cntxt*. If *header* is T, it prefixes the values with a simple header announcing what these are the values of; if other non-NIL value, *header* is printed; otherwise no header at all is printed. If no conclusions were made, prints a message to that effect only if *evenifnil* is set. Since PRINTCONCLUSIONS does not actually make any conclusions, rules with this function in their action will *not* be tried in an attempt to trace the parameter; any such rule should be an *antecedent* rule whose premise insures at the least that the parameter mentioned in the function call has been traced.[4]

```
(PRINTCONCLUSIONS CNTXT DX)
```
Display the bleeding diagnoses of the patient.

A.3 Auxiliary Functions

The following functions are not predicates or conclusions, but may be used to compute arguments to other functions in the premise or action of rules.

LISTOF[*listname*]
    Evaluates its argument; translates as "one of: *listname* ". Usually its argument is the name of a list (which without this function call would have been left unevaluated), but it can also be some expression whose value is a list.

```
(SAME CNTXT SITE (LISTOF STERILESITES))
```
*The site of the culture is **one of**: those sites that are normally sterile.*

ONEOF[*x1, x2, ..., xN*]
    A "no-spread quote": returns its argument list. Used as argument to a basic predicate when a choice of values is indicated. To quote a single value or other type of list, the LISP function QUOTE may be used.

```
(SAME CNTXT SITE (ONEOF URINE SPUTUM))
```
*The site of the culture is **one of**: urine sputum.*

VAL[*cntxt, parm*]
    Returns *parm* of *cntxt* as a list of pairs sorted by decreasing CF: ((value$_1$ cf$_1$) (value$_2$ cf$_2$) ...). VAL traces the parameter if it has not been traced yet.

VAL1[*cntxt, parm* **]**

Similar to **VAL**, but returns only the most highly confirmed value of *parm* of *cntxt* (i.e. the value with the highest CF; the value is returned alone, without the CF). This function only makes sense for single-valued parameters, and is generally only used to obtain the value of a parameter whose value is always known with certainty; in particular, numeric-valued parameters.

MEASURE1[*cntxt, parm* **]**

Similar to **VAL1**, but returns the CF of the most highly confirmed value of *parm* of *cntxt*, rather than the value. Provided for those rare cases where it is necessary to directly manipulate a CF, e.g., to provide a computed CF in a conclusion, or test one explicitly in a premise.

> **(MEASURE1 CNTXT NORMAL)**
> *The measure of certainty associated with whether the organism is normally found at this site.*

GRID[*props, gridname, flg* **]**

Retrieves a static "grid" stored on the property list of *gridname*. *Props*, a list of (*prop, cf*) pairs, is used to index into the grid. Each entry in the grid is a list of (value, cf) pairs. For each (*prop, cf*) pair in *props*, **GRID** retrieves the entry corresponding to *prop* and modifies its cf's by *cf*. The result is one long list of (value, cf) pairs, with the cf's normalized so that the positive ones sum to 1.0; if *flg* is set, no normalization is performed.

GRID1[*prop, gridname* **]**

This is the same as **GRID**, but for just a single *prop* (an atom), retrieving just one entry of the grid.[22]

> **(SAME CNTXT IDENT (LISTOF (GRID1 (VAL1 CNTXT SITE)**
> **NORMAL-FLORA)))**
> *The identity of the organism is one of: **the** normal flora **associated with** the site of the culture.*

TEXT[*label, phrase1, phrase2, ...* **]**

This function is used in the *valu* slot of calls to **CONCLUDETEXT** to construct a value for a text-valued parameter. The first argument is an optional label (or **NIL**) used to tag the value. The remaining arguments are arbitrary forms (generally strings and calls to **TEXTAG**) to construct a text phrase. Result is a list (**TEXT** *label . phrase*). If there is only one argument, the label is interpreted as a text tag, i.e., (**TEXT** *label*) is the same as (**TEXT** *label* (**TEXTAG** *label*)). The optional label is used by **PRINTCONCLUSIONS** to sort conclusions of the same CF; the desired order of the labels is specified as a property **LABEL.ORDER** of the text-valued parameter whose conclusion this is.

TEXTAG[*tag* **]**

This function is used within calls to **TEXT** to quote a text "tag", a place holder for a string of text that is part of the value of a text-valued parameter. *Tag* should be in the system list **TEXTAGS**, and should have a **TRANS**, which is the string to replace references to this tag. Text tags make it easy to refer to the same string in more than one rule.

A.4 Functions for Use in Mapping Rules

The functions described below are used in "mapping rules"—rules that use parameters of each of a specified list of contexts, in addition to parameters of the context to which the rule is normally applied. The functions are divided into three groups: (1) the mapping functions themselves, which appear in a rule's premise and examine selected other contexts, (2) auxiliary functions provided for use within mapping functions, and (3) conclusion functions whose primary use is in conjunction with mapping functions.

Mapping Functions

All of the mapping functions have the arguments *mapset*, *pred*, and *freevar*. They map over the list *mapset* (usually a list of contexts), evaluating *pred* for each element and performing some operation when *pred* is true.[6] *Pred* is a predicate having the same form as a rule premise. *Freevar* is the "iteration variable," local to the mapping function: on each iteration, it is set to the current element of *mapset*.[7] It serves as a context variable in *pred*—it is used to fill the *cntxt* argument of predicates that refer to the context element being mapped over (of course, **CNTXT** is still used inside *pred* to refer to the context to which the rule is being applied). The argument *freevar* is optional; if left **NIL**, the default variable **FREEVAR** is used.

Most of the functions return *anset* set to their result; if not explicitly specified, the default *anset* for **THEREARE**, whose result is a list, is **COLLECTEDLST**, while for the functions that return a single element the default is **FOUNDVAR**. These result variables are global to the clause in which they are computed (but local to the rule); the result of a mapping function in a rule's premise is often used in that rule's action or in later premise clauses.

THEREARE[*mapset, pred, freevar, anset, duples*]
  Collects all the elements of *mapset* for which *pred* is true. If *duples* is T, it returns a list of duples pairing each *freevar* that succeeded with the value (a CF) returned when the predicate *pred* was tested for that element; otherwise it just returns a list of the successful *freevar*'s.

```
(THEREARE (GETALL KNOWNORG)
          ($AND (DEFINITE FREEVAR IDENT))
          NIL COLLECTEDORGS)
```
  You have examined *the organisms isolated from positive cultures obtained from the patient,* **selecting those for which** *the identity of this organism is known with certainty.*
  [Also sets COLLECTEDORGS to the resulting list.]

THEREXISTS[*mapset, pred, freevar, anset*]
  Like THEREARE, but just finds the *first* element (*freevar*) of *mapset* satisfying *pred*, and returns that.

```
(THEREXISTS (GETALL CURTHER)
            ($AND (SAME FREEVAR DNAME (ONEOF AMPICILLIN
                        CARBENICILLIN PENICILLIN METHICILLIN))))
```
  You have examined *current drugs of the patient,* **and have found one for which** *the name of this drug is one of: ampicillin carbenicillin penicillin methicillin.*
  [Also sets FOUNDVAR to the result (a CURTHER context).]

THEREARE![*lst*]
> Returns true if *lst* is non-empty. This is like a call to THEREARE or THEREXISTS with *pred* = T, but translates better, and sets no global variable. Used primarily for checking whether contexts of a certain type exist.

> (THEREARE! (GETOFFSPRING CNTXT SMEARORG))
> **There are** *organisms noted on smears of this culture.*

FORALL[*mapset, pred, freevar*]
> True if *pred* is true for each element of *mapset*. The function returns (trivially) true if *mapset* is empty. Logically speaking, a call to FORALL is the same as
> *not*[THEREXISTS[*mapset, not*[*pred*]*, freevar*].

> (FORALL (GETALL POSCUL)
> ($AND (NOTSAME FREEVAR SPECSTAIN)
> (NOTSAME FREEVAR CRYPTO-SEROLOGY)
> (NOTSAME FREEVAR COCCI-SEROLOGY)))
> *For each of* the positive cultures of the patient *it is true that*
> 1) Organisms were not seen on the stain of this culture,
> 2) The cryptococcal antigen in the csf was not positive, and
> 3) The csf coccidioides serology was not positive

FINDMAX[*mapset, pred, test, freevar, anset*]
> On each iteration, evaluates *test* when *pred* is true. The function returns the *freevar* for which *test* had the largest value. The global variable MAXVAL is set to this maximum value of *test*, and may be used in the rule's **action** or later in the **premise**.

> (FINDMAX (GETALL CURTHER)
> ($AND (KNOWN $FREEDRUG WHENSTART))
> (VAL1 $FREEDRUG WHENSTART)
> $FREEDRUG)
> **You have examined** *the current drugs of the patient* **for which** *the time since therapy with this drug was started is known,* **and have selected the one having the maximum value for** *the time since therapy with this drug was started.*

FINDMIN[*mapset, pred, test, freevar, anset*]
> Like FINDMAX, but looks for the the smallest value of *test*, and sets global MINVAL.

Functions Used within Mapping Functions

The functions **GETALL**, **GETOFFSPRING**, and **APPEND** are used as the *mapset* argument to mapping functions. The predicates **SAMEANS**, **NOTSAMEANS**, and **TRACEDP** are used as clauses within the *pred* argument.

GETALL[*ctype*]
> Returns a list of all contexts of type *ctype*.

GETOFFSPRING[*cntxt, ctype*]
> Like GETALL, but specialized to just one portion of the context tree. Returns a list of descendent contexts of *cntxt* of type *ctype*.

APPEND[*list1, list2, ...*]
　　LISP function that appends its list arguments into one long list. It is used as the *mapset* argument when more than one type of context is to be examined.

SAMEANS[*cntxt1, cntxt2, parm*]
　　Predicate that is true if *cntxt1* and *cntxt2* have the same value for the parameter *parm*. One of *cntxt1* and *cntxt2* is usually CNTXT, and the other the value of the *freevar* argument.

NOTSAMEANS[*cntxt1, cntxt2, parm*]
　　The negation of SAMEANS; i.e., this predicate is true when *cntxt1* and *cntxt2* have *different* values for *parm*.

TRACEDP[*cntxt, parm*]
　　True if *parm* has been traced for *cntxt*. This predicate is generally needed when the value of a parameter of one context is to be transferred to another context. To avoid circular reasoning, the rule specifies that the target parameter is already traced in order for a context to satisfy the mapping predicate.

```
(THEREXISTS (APPEND (GETALL POSCUL) (GETALL PENDCUL))
           ($AND (TRACEDP FREEVAR NOSOCOMIAL)
                 (KNOWN FREEVAR NOSOCOMIAL)
                 (SAMEANS CNTXT FREEVAR SITE))
           NIL FOUNDCUL)
```
You have examined positive cultures obtained from the patient and pending cultures of the patient, and have found one for which
　　　　1) *All information about whether* the infection was acquired while the patient was hospitalized *has been gathered*, and
　　　　2) It is known whether the infection was acquired while the patient was hospitalized, and
　　　　3) The culture under consideration and this culture have the same value for the site of the culture.

Conclusion Functions for Mapping Rules

Sometimes a mapping function is used solely for its value as a predicate (e.g., **FORALL** or **THEREXISTS**), or to compute a simple value to be used in the action (e.g., the **MAXVAL** result of a **FINDMAX** might be used as the *switchnum* argument to **CONCLUDET**). In such cases, the normal conclusion functions are used, though possibly with the inclusion of a variable from the premise. However, more commonly a rule with mapping functions in it wants to manipulate the result of the map in its action in other ways. The following functions are thus provided. Some of the translations are unfortunately awkward, as the task of describing bindings in English is itself awkward.

CONCLIST[*cntxt, parm, valuelist, cf*]
　　Valuelist is a list of duples (value cf), such as returned by VAL or by THEREARE with *duples*=T. Concludes that *parm* of *cntxt* is each of those values, with the certainty of each modified by *cf*.

```
(CONCLIST CNTXT SAMEBUG COLLECTEDORGS 300)
```
　　There is weakly suggestive evidence (.3) that the organisms with possibly the same identity as the organism are each of the organisms that you selected.

CONCLUDEALL[*cntxts, parm, valu, cf*]
   Cntxts is a list of contexts, set by a mapping clause in the rule's **premise**. Makes the same conclusion for each member of the list.

>   (CONCLUDEALL COLLECTEDCULS REQTHER YES -1000)
>   *It is **definite** (1.0) **that** the organisms isolated from the cultures that you selected should not be considered for therapy.*

TRANSPARM[*from, to, parm, cf, positive*]
   Transfers the value of *parm* of context *from* to context *to*, modified by *cf*. Both *from* and *to* may be either a list of contexts or a single context. One of these is generally CNTXT, and the other the result of a mapping function in the **premise** (e.g., COLLECTEDLST or FOUNDVAR). If *positive* is set, only values with positive CF's are transferred.

>   (TRANSPARM FOUNDCUL CNTXT SECONDARY 1000)
>   *It is **definite** (1.0) **that** the **information that you have gathered about** the infection to which the bacteremia is secondary **is also relevant to** this culture.*

TRANSDIFPARM[*from, fparm, to, tparm, cf, positive*]
   Like TRANSPARM, but used when the values to be transferred are associated with two different parameters. *Fparm* and *tparm* must, of course, have the same set of legal values. This function transfers the value of *fparm* of *from* to *tparm* of *to*, modified by *cf*.

>   (TRANSDIFPARM COLLECTEDORGS IDENT CNTXT COVERFOR 700)
>   *There is **suggestive evidence** (.7) **that** the organisms (other than those seen on cultures or smears) which might be causing the infection **are** the identity of **each of** the organisms that you selected.*

TRANSLIST[*from, to, parms, cf*]
   Transfers to context *to* the values of each parameter in *parms* of all contexts in *from*, modifying the CF's of each stored value by *cf*.

>   (TRANSLIST (VAL CNTXT SAMEBUG) CNTXT '(IDENT) 1000)
>   *It is **definite** (1.0) **that** these **properties** — ident — **should be transferred from** the organisms with possibly the same identity as this organism **to** this organism.*

Appendix B

Definition of the Abbreviated Rule Language

This appendix describes the expressions permitted in the abbreviated rule language (ARL). The possibilities provided for in the initial EMYCIN setup are shown in the table below; the designer can extend the set of expressions by defining new operators. The notation used is a modified BNF: meta-symbols are enclosed in angle brackets, terminal symbols are in upper case, alternatives are separated by vertical bars, and expressions inside braces may be repeated ("*" = zero or more times, "+" = one or more times).

⟨premise⟩	→	⟨predicate⟩
⟨action⟩	→	⟨conclusion⟩ {AND ⟨conclusion⟩}*
⟨predicate⟩	→	⟨predicate⟩ AND ⟨predicate⟩ | ⟨predicate⟩ OR ⟨predicate⟩ | ~⟨predicate⟩ |
		⟨ynparm⟩ | ~⟨ynparm⟩ | ⟨parm⟩ = ⟨value⟩ | ⟨parm⟩ ~= ⟨value⟩ |
		⟨parm⟩ IS ⟨isphrase⟩ | ⟨ynparm⟩ IS ⟨samefn⟩ |
		⟨numexp⟩ ⟨numrel⟩ ⟨numexp⟩ | ⟨lispform⟩
⟨isphrase⟩	→	KNOWN | NOTKNOWN | DEFINITE | NOTDEFINITE |
		DEFINITELY ⟨value⟩ | DEFINITELY NOT ⟨value⟩ | ⟨samefn⟩ ⟨value⟩
⟨samefn⟩	→	THOUGHTNOT | MIGHTBE | VNOTKNOWN |
		DEFIS | DEFNOT | NOTDEFIS | NOTDEFNOT
⟨numexp⟩	→	⟨number⟩ | ⟨numparm⟩ |
		⟨numexp⟩ ⟨numop⟩ ⟨numexp⟩ | -⟨numexp⟩ | ⟨lispform⟩
⟨numop⟩	→	+ | - | * | / | ↑
⟨numrel⟩	→	< | > | <= | >=
⟨conclusion⟩	→	⟨ynparm⟩ ⟨cf⟩ | ~⟨ynparm⟩ ⟨cf⟩ |
		⟨parm⟩ = ⟨value⟩ ⟨cf⟩ | ⟨parm⟩ ~= ⟨value⟩ ⟨cf⟩ | ⟨parm⟩ = ⟨valuelist⟩ |
		⟨parm⟩ = ⟨parm⟩ | ⟨parm⟩ = TABLE | ⟨lispform⟩
⟨valuelist⟩	→	{⟨atomvalue⟩ ⟨numcf⟩}⁺
⟨cf⟩	→	⟨numcf⟩ | (⟨numcf⟩) | *null*
⟨numcf⟩	→	*a number in the range* [−1, 1]
⟨parm⟩	→	*a parameter*
⟨ynparm⟩	→	*a yes/no parameter*
⟨numparm⟩	→	*a numeric-valued parameter*
⟨value⟩	→	⟨atomvalue⟩ | ⟨lispform⟩
⟨atomvalue⟩	→	*an atomic value for a parameter*
⟨lispform⟩	→	*a variable or a LISP expression:* $(function\ arg_1\ arg_2\ ...)$
⟨number⟩	→	*a number*

Subexpressions may be grouped by parentheses (this was not stated explicitly in the syntax description above, for readability). In the absence of parentheses, the precedence of the operators is listed below, in decreasing order; operators of the same precedence are evaluated left to right. The only nonstandard precedence is that of **AND** and **OR**, which is reversed (since all rule premises are conjunctions, **AND** has lowest precedence).

$$unary \ -$$
$$\uparrow$$
$$* \ and \ /$$
$$+ \ and \ -$$

all relational operators $(<, \ >, \ =, \ etc.)$

$$\sim$$
OR
AND

GT, **LT**, **GE**, and **LE** are synonyms for the relations $>$, $<$, $>=$, and $<=$, respectively; " , " (comma) is a synonym for **AND**. In the case of most single-character operators ($=$, $+$, $*$, etc.), the operator may appear embedded in a large atom or separated by spaces from its operands; the exceptions are the operators "-" and "/", which are commonly used as separators inside parameter and value names, and therefore must be delimited by blanks to prevent ambiguity.[1]

LISP and ARL may be freely intermixed. Ordinary LISP forms may appear most any place that a computed operand is allowed; conversely, ARL forms, in parentheses, may be used as arguments to LISP functions.

In all forms that use a context, the variable **CNTXT** is assumed.[2] A yes/no parameter (⟨ynparm⟩) standing alone as a predicate or conclusion has the meaning of "⟨ynparm⟩ = **YES**"; "∼⟨ynparm⟩" means "⟨ynparm⟩ ∼= **YES**." A numeric-valued parameter (⟨numparm⟩) used as operand in an arithmetic expression stands for "(**VAL1 CNTXT** ⟨numparm⟩)." If a numeric expression involves only one parameter, whose units are known, then any numbers in the same expression can be qualified with a unit of measure; for example, the following is permissible:

$$AGE > 9 \ MONTHS,$$

which would be converted to (**GREATERP*** (**VAL1 CNTXT AGE**) .75).

In conclusions, the operator "$=$" has several possible meanings. The most common, in "⟨parm⟩ = value⟩," is for the function **CONCLUDE**. If the parameter is text-valued, the function is **CONCLUDETEXT**, and the ⟨value⟩ is taken to be a call to **TEXT**. Other cases are shown below. If a CF for a conclusion is omitted, the CF is taken to be 1.0 (definite).

The following table shows expressions using each of the ARL operators, and the corresponding LISP forms into which they translate. This table does not cover all the possibilities, but is intended as a guide.

ARL	LISP

Predicates:

parm = *value*	(SAME CNTXT *parm value*)
parm ~= *value*	(NOTSAME CNTXT *parm value*)
ynparm	(SAME CNTXT *ynparm*)
~*ynparm*	(NOTSAME CNTXT *ynparm*)
parm IS KNOWN	(KNOWN CNTXT *parm*)

(*similarly for* NOTKNOWN, DEFINITE, NOTDEFINITE)

parm IS DEFINITELY *value*	(DEFIS CNTXT *parm value*)
parm IS DEFINITELY NOT *value*	(DEFNOT CNTXT *parm value*)
parm IS THOUGHTNOT *value*	(THOUGHTNOT CNTXT *parm value*)

(*similarly for* MIGHTBE, VNOTKNOWN, DEFIS, DEFNOT, NOTDEFIS, NOTDEFNOT)

ynparm IS THOUGHTNOT	(THOUGHTNOT CNTXT *ynparm*)

(*similarly for* MIGHTBE, DEFIS, DEFNOT, NOTDEFIS, NOTDEFNOT)

numexp1 > *numexp2*	(GREATERP* *numexp1 numexp2*)

(*similarly for the other arithmetic relations:* < → LESSP*, >= → GREATEQ*, <= → LESSEQ*)

~*predicate*	($NOT *predicate*)
pred1 AND *pred2* AND ...	($AND *pred1 pred2* ...)
pred1 OR *pred2* OR ...	($OR *pred1 pred2* ...)

Numeric Expressions:

numparm (as an operand)	(VAL1 CNTXT *numparm*)
numexp1 + *numexp2* + ...	(PLUS *numexp1 numexp2* ...)
numexp1 * *numexp2* * ...	(TIMES *numexp1 numexp2* ...)
numexp1 - *numexp2*	(DIFFERENCE *numexp1 numexp2*)
numexp1 / *numexp2*	(FQUOTIENT *numexp1 numexp2*)
numexp1 ↑ *numexp2*	(EXPT *numexp1 numexp2*)
- *numexp*	(MINUS *numexp*)

Conclusions:

parm = *value* (*cf*)	(CONCLUDE CNTXT *parm value* TALLY *cf*)
parm = *value*	(CONCLUDE CNTXT *parm value* TALLY 1000)
parm ~= *value* (*cf*)	(CONCLUDE CNTXT *parm value* TALLY -*cf*)
ynparm (*cf*)	(CONCLUDE CNTXT *ynparm* YES TALLY *cf*)
~*ynparm* (*cf*)	(CONCLUDE CNTXT *ynparm* NO TALLY *cf*)
parm = *value1 cf1 value2 cf2* ...	(CONCLUDE* CNTXT *parm* TALLY '((*value1 cf1*) (*value2 cf2*) ...))
textparm = *textag* (*cf*)	(CONCLUDETEXT CNTXT *textparm* (TEXT *textag*) TALLY *cf*)
parm1 = *parm2* (*cf*)	(TRANSDIFPARM CNTXT *parm2* CNTXT *parm1 cf*)
parm = TABLE	(CONCLUDET CNTXT *switch cases* TALLY *parm values*), with switch, cases and values filled in by an interactive routine.

Appendix C

Definition of the Control Structure

This appendix describes the main portion of the EMYCIN control structure in an informal ALGOL-style set of procedures. The procedure names have been chosen to be suggestive of each procedure's task. The procedure *TraceParameter*, for example, defines what it means to "trace a parameter of a context." The consultation begins with the call *InstantiateContext* (**null**, *TreeRoot*), where *TreeRoot* denotes the root node of the context type hierarchy. Those procedures that are not defined here are considered primitives.

To reduce clutter, block nesting is depicted graphically by level of indentation, rather than by explicit **begin-end** pairs. The informal datatypes declared for variables are purely for documentation. They are all entities described in Chapter 2, or composites of such entities; e.g., **valuelist** is a list of (**value, cf**) pairs. The variables *cntxt* and *parm* are implicitly of types **context** and **parameter**. The declaration "**default** =" designates a default value to use when the corresponding procedure argument is omitted from a procedure call. The syntax "*variable:*FIELD" denotes an operation to access FIELD of *variable*, viewing *variable* as a record structure (most of these are implemented in EMYCIN as property-list operations). For logical constructs, the value of a non-Boolean item is considered **false** if it is **null** or is a **cf** less than or equal to .2; **true** otherwise. The arguments to all procedures are passed by value only.

procedure *TraceParameter* (*cntxt, parm*)
    comment Determine the value of *parm* of *cntxt.*

    declare *onerule* **rule**
    if *onerule* ← *FindUnitypath* (*cntxt, parm*)
      then *ApplyRule* (*onerule, cntxt*)
      else **if** *parm:*ASKFIRST
            then *AskForParameter* (*cntxt, parm*)
                if ~ *IsTraced* (*cntxt, parm*)
                    then **comment** Answer was **unknown** or less than certain.
                          InferParameter (*cntxt, parm*)
          else *InferParameter* (*cntxt, parm*)
              if ~ *Known* (*cntxt, parm*)
                  then *AskForParameter* (*cntxt, parm*)
    AssertTraced (*cntxt, parm*)

procedure *AskForParameter* (*cntxt, parm*)
    comment If *parm* is askable, obtains its value by asking the client.

    declare *answers* **valuelist**
    if *parm:*PROMPT **is not null**
      and *parm:*MULTIVALUED ≠ T
      and ~ *MarkedAsUnaskable* (*cntxt,parm*)
    then *answers* ← *AskClient* (*cntxt, parm*)
          if *answers* ≠ **unknown**
              then **for** [*value, cf*] ∈ *answers* **do** *Conclude* (*cntxt, parm, value, cf*)

procedure *InferParameter* (*cntxt, parm*)
    comment Uses rules to determine the value of *parm* of *cntxt.*

    declare *rules* **list of rules**
    rules ← *RulesThatConclude* (*parm*)
    rules ← *ApplyMetaRules* (*rules, cntxt, parm*)
    for *R* ∈ *rules*
      do **if** *Applicable* (*R, cntxt*)
             then *ApplyRule* (*R, cntxt*)
             else **for** *ctype* ∈ *ApplicableTypes* (*rule*)
                    do **for** *subcontext* ∈ *FindDescendentsOf* (*cntxt, ctype*)
                          do *ApplyRule* (*rule, subcontext*)
      until *IsTraced* (*cntxt, parm*)

procedure *ApplyRule* (*CurrentRule, Cntxt*)
    comment Applies *CurrentRule* to *Cntxt.* The variable *Cntxt* is used freely inside the rule
        evaluation.

    declare *CurrentRule* **rule**
    if *Preview* (*CurrentRule*)
      then **comment** The rule is already known to fail.
      else **if** *Evaluate* (*CurrentRule:*PREMISE)
             then *Evaluate* (*CurrentRule:*ACTION)

procedure *FindDescendentsOf*(*cntxt, ctype*) **returns list of contexts**
 comment Returns a list of all descendent contexts of *cntxt* of type *ctype*, instantiating them if they haven't been yet.

 declare *ctype* **context-type**
 while there are more uninstantiated descendents of *cntxt* of type *ctype*
  do *InstantiateContext* (*cntxt, ctype*)
 return *ListofDescendentsOf*(*cntxt, ctype*)

procedure *InstantiateContext* (*parentcontext, ctype*)
 comment Creates a new instance of context type *ctype*, a descendent of *parentcontext*.

 declare *parentcontext, cntxt* **context**; *ctype* **context-type**
 cntxt ← *CreateNewContext* (*ctype*)
 if *parentcontext* ≠ **null**
  then *cntxt:*PARENT ← *parentcontext*
    append *cntxt* **to** *ListofDescendentsOf*(*parentcontext, ctype*)
 for *parm* ∈ *ctype:*INITIALDATA **do** *TraceParameter* (*cntxt, parm*)
 for *parm* ∈ *ctype:*GOALS **do** *TraceParameter* (*cntxt, parm*)

procedure *Conclude* (*cntxt, parm, value, cf, tally*)
 comment Standard call in the action of a rule. *Tally* is the certainty of the premise.

 declare *value* **value**; *cf* **cf**; *tally* **cf default** = 1.0; *triple* **fact-triple**
 cf ← *cf* × *tally*
 if *triple* ← *LookUpTriple* (*cntxt, parm, value*)
  then comment Update the CF of the existing triple.
    *triple:*CF ← *CfCombine* (*triple:*CF, *cf*)
  else *StoreNewTriple* (*cntxt, parm, value, cf*)
 if ~*parm:*MULTIVALUED
  and (*cf* = 1 **or** (*IsYesnoParameter* (*parm*) **and** *cf* = −1))
  then comment Parameter is known with certainty, thereby excluding other values.
    AssertTraced (*cntxt, parm*)

procedure *AssertTraced* (*cntxt, parm*)
 comment Called when we have found out everything about *parm* of *cntxt*.

 if ~*IsTraced* (*cntxt, parm*)
  then *MarkAsTraced* (*cntxt, parm*)
    for *R* ∈ *AntecedentRulesOf*(*parm*)
     do if *EntirelyKnown* (*R:*PREMISE) **and** *Evaluate* (*R:*PREMISE) **is true**
       then *Evaluate* (*R:*ACTION)

procedure *$AND* (*clauselist*) **returns cf**
 comment This procedure is called by the premise of every rule. Computes the CF of the conjunction of its clause arguments.

```
declare clauselist list of rule-clauses; result, clausevalue cf
result ← 1.0
for clause ∈ clauselist
    do   clausevalue ← Evaluate (clause)
         if clausevalue ≤ .2
             then  comment  The clause failed.
                   return 0
             else  result ← min (result, clausevalue)
return result
```

procedure *FindValueOf*(*cntxt*, *parm*) **returns valuelist**
   comment Called by SAME, VAL and other procedures needing the value of *parm* of *cntxt*. This is
   the way in which parameters usually become traced.

```
if ~IsTraced (cntxt, parm)
    then  if IsBeingTraced (cntxt, parm)
              then  comment  This is a case of circular reasoning (an error).
                    AbortRule (CurrentRule)
              else  TraceParameter (cntxt, parm)
return LookUpValueOf (cntxt, parm)
```

procedure *Preview* (*rule*) **returns Boolean**
   comment Returns true if *rule* is already known to fail for the current context.

```
for clause ∈ ClausesOf (rule:PREMISE)
    do  if EntirelyKnown (clause) and Evaluate (clause) is false
            then return true
return false
```

procedure *FindUnityPath* (*cntxt*, *parm*, *value*) **returns rule**
   comment Looks for a rule to conclude that *cntxt* of *parm* is definitely *value* on the basis of what is
   known now.

```
declare value value default = any
for rule ∈ RulesThatConclude (parm)
    do  if Applicable (rule, cntxt)
        and CertaintyFactorIn (rule:ACTION) = 1.0
        and [value = any or ValueIn (rule:ACTION) = value]
        and [for clause ∈ ClausesOf (rule:PREMISE) always IsDefinitelyTrue (clause)]
            then return rule
return null
```

procedure *IsDefinitelyTrue* (*clause*) **returns Boolean**
   comment True if *clause* is known to be true with certainty, or can be proved true with certainty.

declare *clause* **rule-clause**
   return (if *EntirelyKnown* (*clause*)
        then *Evaluate* (*clause*) = 1.0
        elseif *clause* is of the form *"parm = value"*
        then **comment** Try to establish that *parm* is definitely *value.*
           FindUnityPath (*cntxt, parm, value*))

The following are declarations for some of the procedures not spelled out in full:

procedure *AbortRule* (*rule*) **does not return**
   comment Returns control to *ApplyRule*, ignoring intervening procedure calls, with an indication that *rule* failed due to circular reasoning.

procedure *AskClient* (*cntxt, parm*) **returns valuelist**
   comment Asks the client for the value of *parm* of *cntxt*, using a suitable prompt. Parses the client's response, handling any special commands, and returns a list of (value, cf) pairs (usually just one), or **unknown**.

procedure *ApplicableTypes* (*rule*) **returns list of context-types**
   comment Returns a list of context types to which *rule* could be applied.

procedure *ApplyMetaRules* (*rulelist, cntxt, parm*) **returns list of rules**
   comment Reorders and/or prunes *rulelist* by applying any metarules relevant to *parm* of *cntxt*.

procedure *CfCombine* (*cf1, cf2*) **returns cf**
   comment Computes the combined certainty factor for two conclusions about the same context, parameter and value (see page 41).

procedure *EntirelyKnown* (*clause*) **returns Boolean**
   comment True if every context/parameter pair in *clause* is already traced.

procedure *LookUpValueOf* (*cntxt, parm*) **returns valuelist**
   comment Returns a list of (value, cf) pairs, one for each value concluded for *parm* of *cntxt* (i.e., one for each triple containing *cntxt* and *parm*).

To keep the description above simple, some bookkeeping details have been omitted, notably the records kept for the explanation system. In addition, if it is possible to have rules that conclude about more than one parameter (which EMYCIN allows), then *ApplyRule* and *AssertTraced* need to make sure that the rules they apply have not already been applied to the selected context. *FindUnityPath* needs to have an extra check to prevent looping in cases of circular reasoning.

Appendix D

Examples of Rule Compiler Output

Two examples are given here of the compilation of rule sets from the MYCIN knowledge base. Each example lists the original rules, the tree into which RCOMPL transforms the rules, and the resulting LISP code. The first example is short and illustrates the general nature of the code emitted; the second example is somewhat longer and illustrates the way in which certainty factors are compiled.

For readability, the rules and tree are stated in ARL, with the parameters and values in uppercase; see Appendix B for the LISP forms that are equivalent to the ARL expressions.

D.1 Example 1—NORMAL

The following four rules conclude the parameter **NORMAL** (*the organism is normally found at this site*).

```
RULE087
  If:  1) SITE = (LISTOF NONSTERILESITES),
       2) IDENT is definite, and
       3) IDENT = (LISTOF (GRID1 (VAL1 CNTXT SITE)
                                 NORMAL-FLORA))
  Then:  NORMAL = YES (1.0)


RULE355
  If:  1) SITE = URETHRA,
       2) SEX = MALE, and
       3) IDENT is definitely (ONEOF CORYNEBACTERIUM-NON-DIPHTHERIAE MYCOPLASMA)
  Then:  NORMAL = YES (.5)


RULE389
  If:  1) SITE = URETHRA,
       2) SEX = MALE, and
       3) IDENT is definitely STAPHYLOCOCCUS-COAG-NEG
  Then:  NORMAL = YES (.8)


RULE390
  If:  1) SITE = URETHRA,
       2) SEX = FEMALE, and
       3) IDENT is definitely MYCOPLASMA
  Then:  NORMAL = YES (.2)
```

The rule compiler converts that set of rules into the following decision tree:

```
if SITE = (LISTOF NONSTERILESITES)
then
   if IDENT is definite
   then
      if SITE = URETHRA
      then if SEX = FEMALE
            then if IDENT is definitely MYCOPLASMA
                  then {conclusion of RULE390}
            else if SEX = MALE¹
                  then if IDENT is definitely STAPHYLOCOCCUS-COAG-NEG
                        then {conclusion of RULE389}
                        else if IDENT is definitely
                                    (ONEOF CORYNEBACTERIUM-NON-DIPHTHERIAE
                                           MYCOPLASMA)
                        then {conclusion of RULE355}
   if IDENT = (LISTOF (GRID1 (VAL1 CNTXT SITE) NORMAL-FLORA))
   then {conclusion of RULE087}
```

The LISP function produced as output of RCOMPL is shown below. This function is passed to the INTERLISP compiler, which converts it to machine code that can be executed in place of the original four rules. For an explanation of the variables and functions used in this code, see the glossary following the second example (page 150).

```
[LAMBDA NIL
  (PROG ((CUL-CNTXT (SUBVAL CNTXT 'SITE))
         TALLY #2 #1)
        [COND
          ((FMEMB (SETQ #2 (CAAR (VAL CUL-CNTXT 'SITE T)))
                  NONSTERILESITES)
            (PROG ((CURULE 'RULE087))
              (COND
                ((EQ (CADAR (VAL CNTXT 'IDENT T))
                     1000)
                  [COND
                    ((EQ #2 'URETHRA)
                      (COND
                        [(EQ (SETQ #1 (CAAR (VAL ROOTNODE 'SEX T)))
                             'FEMALE)
                          (PROG ((CURULE 'RULE390))
                            (COND
                              ((EQ (SAME CNTXT 'IDENT 'MYCOPLASMA T)
                                   1000)
                                (CONCLUDE CNTXT 'NORMAL 'YES 1000 200 T)
                                (SETAPPL]
                        (T
                          (COND
                            ((EQ #1 'MALE)
                              (COND
                                ((EQ (SAME CNTXT 'IDENT 'STAPHYLOCOCCUS-COAG-NEG T)
                                     1000)
                                  (PROG ((CURULE 'RULE389))
                                    (CONCLUDE CNTXT 'NORMAL 'YES 1000 800 T)
                                    (SETAPPL)))
                                (T (PROG ((CURULE 'RULE355))
                                    (COND
                                      ((EQ (SAME CNTXT 'IDENT
                                                 '(CORYNEBACTERIUM-NON-DIPHTHERIAE
                                                   MYCOPLASMA)
                                                 T)
                                           1000)
```

```
                                   (CONCLUDE CNTXT 'NORMAL 'YES 1000 500
                                       T)
                                   (SETAPPL]
                       (COND
                           ((TALLYP1 (SETQ TALLY (SAME CNTXT 'IDENT (GETPROP 'NORMAL-FLORA
                                                                                  #2)
                                       T)))
                           (CONCLUDE CNTXT 'NORMAL 'YES TALLY 1000 T)
                           (SETAPPL T]
           (RETURN)
       RULEXIT
           (RETURN T]
```

D.2 Example 2—AIR

The following 11 rules make up one block of the rule set to conclude the parameter **AIR**
(*the aerobicity of the organism*).

RULE027
　If:　1) SITE = BLOOD,
　　　2) AIRGROW, and
　　　3) ANGROW
　Then:　AIR = FACUL (.8),
　　　　　ANAEROBIC (.2)

RULE028
　If:　1) AIRGROW is mightbe,
　　　2) ANTRY, and
　　　3) ANGROW is thoughtnot
　Then:　AIR = OBLIGATE-AEROB (.7),
　　　　　FACUL (.3)

RULE029
　If:　1) AIRGROW is thoughtnot,
　　　2) SITE = BLOOD or ANTRY, and
　　　3) ANGROW
　Then:　AIR = ANAEROBIC (.8),
　　　　　FACUL (.3)

RULE128
　If:　1) AIRGROW,
　　　2) SITE = BLOOD or ANTRY, and
　　　3) ANGROW is not known
　Then:　AIR = OBLIGATE-AEROB (.4),
　　　　　FACUL (.4), ANAEROBIC (.2)

RULE129
　If:　1) AIRGROW is thoughtnot,
　　　2) SITE = BLOOD or ANTRY, and
　　　3) ANGROW is not known
　Then:　AIR = ANAEROBIC (.7), FACUL (.3)

RULE130
　If:　1) SITE ~= BLOOD,
　　　2) AIRGROW is not known, and
　　　3) ~ANTRY
　Then:　AIR = FACUL (.5), ANAEROBIC (.2),
　　　　　OBLIGATE-AEROB (.3)

RULE334
　If:　1) AIRGROW is not known,
　　　2) SITE = BLOOD or ANTRY, and
　　　3) ANGROW
　Then:　AIR = FACUL (.5),
　　　　　ANAEROBIC (.5)

RULE335
　If:　1) SITE ~= BLOOD,
　　　2) AIRGROW,
　　　3) ANTRY, and
　　　4) ANGROW
　Then:　AIR = FACUL (1.0)

RULE337
　If:　1) SITE ~= BLOOD,
　　　2) AIRGROW, and
　　　3) ~ANTRY
　Then:　AIR = OBLIGATE-AEROB (.4),
　　　　　FACUL (.4), ANAEROBIC (.2)

RULE338
　If:　1) SITE ~= BLOOD,
　　　2) AIRGROW is thoughtnot, and
　　　3) ~ANTRY
　Then:　AIR = ANAEROBIC (.7),
　　　　　FACUL (.3)

RULE357
　If:　1) AIRGROW is not known,
　　　2) SITE = BLOOD or ANTRY, and
　　　3) ANGROW is not known
　Then:　AIR = FACUL (.5),
　　　　　OBLIGATE-AEROB (.3),
　　　　　ANAEROBIC (.2)

The resulting decision tree is as follows:

```
if AIRGROW²⁸
  then if ANGROW
        then if SITE = BLOOD
                then {conclusion of RULE027}
                else if ANTRY²⁹
                        then {conclusion of RULE335}
        else if 1) ANGROW is not known, and
                2) SITE = BLOOD or ANTRY
             then {conclusion of RULE128}
        if 1) SITE ~= BLOOD, and
           2) ~ANTRY
        then {conclusion of RULE337}
  else if AIRGROW is not known
        then if SITE = BLOOD or ANTRY
                then if ANGROW
                        then {conclusion of RULE334}
                        else if ANGROW is not known
                                then {conclusion of RULE357}
                else {conclusion of RULE130}
        else if SITE = BLOOD or ANTRY
                then if ANGROW
                        then {conclusion of RULE029}
                        else if ANGROW is not known
                                then {conclusion of RULE129}
                else {conclusion of RULE338}
  if 1) AIRGROW is mightbe,
     2) ANTRY, and
     3) ANGROW is thoughtnot
  then {conclusion of RULE028}
```

The LISP function resulting from this tree is shown on the next page.

```
[LAMBDA NIL
  (PROG (TALLY NEWTALLY (CUL-CNTXT (SUBVAL CNTXT 'SITE))
               #2 #1)
        [COND
          [[TALLYP1 (SETQ TALLY (SETQ #2 (TOPCFOF (VAL CNTXT 'AIRGROW T]
            [COND
              [[TALLYP1 (SETQ NEWTALLY (SETQ #1 (TOPCFOF (VAL CNTXT 'ANGROW T]
                (PROG ((TALLY (MINTALLY TALLY NEWTALLY)))
                      (COND
                        ((EQ (CAAR (VAL CUL-CNTXT 'SITE T))
                             'BLOOD)
                          (PROG ((CURULE 'RULE027))
                                (CONCLUDE CNTXT 'AIR 'FACUL TALLY 800 T)
                                (CONCLUDE CNTXT 'AIR 'ANAEROBIC TALLY 200 T)
                                (SETAPPL)))
                        (T (PROG ((CURULE 'RULE335))
                                 (COND
                                   ([TALLYP1 (SETQ NEWTALLY (TOPCFOF
                                                           (VAL CNTXT 'ANTRY T]
                                     (CONCLUDE CNTXT 'AIR 'FACUL (MINTALLY TALLY
                                                                          NEWTALLY)
                                               1000 T)
                                     (SETAPPL T]
              (T (PROG ((CURULE 'RULE128))
                       (COND
                         ([AND (NOT (TALLYP1 (IABS #1)))
                           (OR (AND (EQ (CAAR (VAL CUL-CNTXT 'SITE T))
                                        'BLOOD)
                                    (SETQ NEWTALLY 1000))
                               (TALLYP1 (SETQ NEWTALLY (TOPCFOF
                                                       (VAL CNTXT 'ANTRY T]
                           (CONCLUDE CNTXT 'AIR 'OBLIGATE-AEROB (SETQ #1
                                         (MINTALLY TALLY NEWTALLY))
                                     400 T)
                           (CONCLUDE CNTXT 'AIR 'FACUL #1 400 T)
                           (CONCLUDE CNTXT 'AIR 'ANAEROBIC #1 200 T)
                           (SETAPPL]
              (PROG ((CURULE 'RULE337))
                    (COND
                      ([AND (NOT (EQ (CAAR (VAL CUL-CNTXT 'SITE T))
                                     'BLOOD))
                        (NOT (TALLYP1 (TOPCFOF (VAL CNTXT 'ANTRY T]
                        (CONCLUDE CNTXT 'AIR 'OBLIGATE-AEROB TALLY 400 T)
                        (CONCLUDE CNTXT 'AIR 'FACUL TALLY 400 T)
                        (CONCLUDE CNTXT 'AIR 'ANAEROBIC TALLY 200 T)
                        (SETAPPL]
          (T (COND
               [(NOT (TALLYP1 (IABS #2)))
                 (PROG ((CURULE 'RULE334))
                       (COND
                         [[OR (AND (EQ (CAAR (VAL CUL-CNTXT 'SITE T))
                                       'BLOOD)
                                   (SETQ TALLY 1000))
                           (TALLYP1 (SETQ TALLY (TOPCFOF (VAL CNTXT 'ANTRY T]
                           (COND
                             [[TALLYP1 (SETQ NEWTALLY (SETQ #1
                                             (TOPCFOF (VAL CNTXT 'ANGROW T]
                               (PROG ((TALLY (MINTALLY TALLY NEWTALLY)))
                                     (PROGN (CONCLUDE CNTXT 'AIR 'FACUL TALLY 500 T)
                                            (CONCLUDE CNTXT 'AIR 'ANAEROBIC TALLY 500
                                                      T)
                                     (SETAPPL]
                             (T (PROG ((CURULE 'RULE357))
                                      (COND
                                        ((NOT (TALLYP1 (IABS #1)))
                                          (CONCLUDE CNTXT 'AIR 'FACUL TALLY 500 T)
                                          (CONCLUDE CNTXT 'AIR 'ANAEROBIC TALLY 200 T)
```

```
                              (CONCLUDE CNTXT 'AIR 'OBLIGATE-AEROB TALLY
                                                                  300 T)
                              (SETAPPL]
                    (T (PROG ((CURULE 'RULE130))
                          (CONCLUDE CNTXT 'AIR 'FACUL 1000 500 T)
                          (CONCLUDE CNTXT 'AIR 'ANAEROBIC 1000 200 T)
                          (CONCLUDE CNTXT 'AIR 'OBLIGATE-AEROB 1000 300 T)
                          (SETAPPL]
          (T (TALLYP1 (SETQ TALLY (IMINUS #2)))
                (PROG ((CURULE 'RULE029))
                    (COND
                      [[OR (AND (EQ (CAAR (VAL CUL-CNTXT 'SITE T))
                                        'BLOOD)
                                   (SETQ NEWTALLY 1000))
                            (TALLYP1 (SETQ NEWTALLY (TOPCFOF (VAL CNTXT
                                                                'ANTRY T]
                        (PROG ((TALLY (MINTALLY TALLY NEWTALLY)))
                            (COND
                              [[TALLYP1 (SETQ NEWTALLY
                                          (SETQ #1 (TOPCFOF (VAL CNTXT
                                                                'ANGROW T]
                                (PROG ((TALLY (MINTALLY TALLY NEWTALLY)))
                                    (PROGN (CONCLUDE CNTXT 'AIR 'FACUL TALLY
                                                                  300 T)
                                        (CONCLUDE CNTXT 'AIR 'ANAEROBIC
                                                              TALLY 800 T)
                                        (SETAPPL]
                            (T (PROG ((CURULE 'RULE129))
                                (COND
                                  ((NOT (TALLYP1 (IABS #1)))
                                    (CONCLUDE CNTXT 'AIR 'FACUL TALLY 300
                                                            T)
                                    (CONCLUDE CNTXT 'AIR 'ANAEROBIC TALLY
                                                            700 T)
                                    (SETAPPL]
                      (T (PROG ((CURULE 'RULE338))
                            (CONCLUDE CNTXT 'AIR 'FACUL TALLY 300 T)
                            (CONCLUDE CNTXT 'AIR 'ANAEROBIC TALLY 700 T)
                            (SETAPPL]
      [PROG ((CURULE 'RULE028))
            (COND
              ([AND (NOT (SLESSP #2 -200))
                    [TALLYP1 (SETQ TALLY (TOPCFOF (VAL CNTXT 'ANTRY T]
                    (AND.TALLY TALLY TALLY1
                            (TALLYP1 (SETQ TALLY1
                                        (IMINUS (TOPCFOF (VAL CNTXT 'ANGROW T]
                (CONCLUDE CNTXT 'AIR 'FACUL TALLY 300 T)
                (CONCLUDE CNTXT 'AIR 'OBLIGATE-AEROB TALLY 700 T)
                (SETAPPL]
      (RETURN)
  RULEXIT
      (RETURN T]
```

D.3 Glossary for the Examples

Variables

CNTXT—the context to which the rule is being applied.

ROOTNODE—(global variable) The root node of the context tree; in MYCIN, this is the node that corresponds to the patient. RCOMPL replaces **CNTXT** with **ROOTNODE** when it knows that the parameter being referenced is a parameter of the root context.

CURULE—(special variable) The "current rule," i.e., the one currently being evaluated.

The rule interpreter binds this variable in order to provide this information to the explanation program, among others. The code emitted by RCOMPL binds CURULE to (some) rule containing the clause that is being tested at any branch, if there is any chance that the branch will cause tracing.

TALLY—(local variable) Maintains the minimum CF of any clause in the premise, to be used to modify the certainty of the conclusion.

NEWTALLY—(local variable) Used as a second variable in some CF computations.

#1, etc.—(local variables) Generated by the common subexpression eliminator to store shared values temporarily.

Functions and Macros

All functions in the output code not mentioned explicitly here are either EMYCIN functions (Appendix A) or LISP functions.

SUBVAL[*cntxt, parm*]
Implements the binding mechanism of the context tree. Searches up the context tree starting at *cntxt* and returns the node to which *parm* could apply. **SUBVAL** is ordinarily called by all functions used in rules that need to access parameters of **CNTXT**. These multiple calls to **SUBVAL** are suppressed (by an extra argument to **VAL**, **SAME**, and a few other functions) in code emitted by RCOMPL, because RCOMPL has already determined the correct bindings.

The following are compiler macros:

TOPCFOF[*valuelist*]
Returns the CF associated with the most highly confirmed value in *valuelist*, a list of the type returned by **VAL**; returns zero if *valuelist* is **NIL**.

TALLYP1[*cf*]
A predicate that is true if *cf* is in the "true" range, i.e., CF $>.2$.

MINTALLY[*tally1, tally2*]
Returns the smaller of the two "tally variables" *tally1* and *tally2*.

SETAPPL[*flag*]
Sets the record indicating that the current rule was successfully applied. In addition, if *flag* is true, tests to see whether the parameter whose tracing invoked this block of rules is now traced, and if so, exits the block, returning **T** (see Section 5.3.3).

AND.TALLY[*maintally, subtally, predicate*]
Used to implement **$AND**. *Predicate* is a LISP predicate that returns true or false, but as a side effect sets the variable *subtally* to a CF corresponding to the CF that would be returned by an EMYCIN predicate in a **$AND**. The value of **AND.TALLY** is the value of *predicate* (true or false in the LISP sense), but as a side effect when the predicate is true it sets *maintally* to the smaller of *maintally* and *subtally*. This slightly awkward form was chosen in order to allow optimization of the code that carries **TALLY** down the tree.

Notes

1. "Essential MYCIN," i.e., MYCIN stripped of its domain knowledge. EMYCIN is in no way related to E-Mycin®, a registered trademark of The Upjohn Company for a form of the drug erythromycin.

2. The system designer may not actually be the domain expert, and more commonly is an intermediary for the expert. More on this in Chapter 6.

3. The terse prompts are standard abbreviations for the set of coagulation screen tests: *PT* is the prothrombin time; *PTT* the activated partial thromboplastin time; *PC* the platelet count; *BT* the bleeding time; *TT* the thrombin time; *FSF* the urea solubility.

4. It should be noted that Mr. Bennett had prior experience with EMYCIN (notably in developing SACON), and thus was far from a naive user. Also, the version described here is but a preliminary version. However, we still find encouraging the speed with which this latest consultation system was produced.

5. Historically, the motivation for this arose from Waterman's success in keeping his program's knowledge base in explicit data structures to facilitate modifications [Waterman 70], and from DENDRAL's success at separating the knowledge base from the inference mechanism. See [Shortliffe 74] for a discussion of other design goals for MYCIN.

6. This general scheme was tried in MYCIN and discarded because the resulting question order was confusing; this concern led to the development of the context tree.

Notes for Chapter 2

1. These two triples could also be thought of as *one* triple in which the **value** part is a list of alternative values, and each CF is associated with a value. The two forms are logically equivalent, and we will speak of them in the form that is most convenient for the particular discussion. A set of triples for a given context/parameter pair is, in fact, represented internally as a list of (value, cf) pairs stored on the property list of the context under the property named by the parameter. The fact that triples are indexed by context/parameter and thus are not at all symmetric influences how they may be manipulated; e.g., it is much easier to ask "what is the identity of Organism 1?" than "what organisms have identity Pseudomonas?"

2. Incidentally, since CF's are not probabilities, there is no requirement that the CF's for the values of a given context and parameter sum to 1 (or less).

3. For reasons of efficiency in the INTERLISP implementation, CF's are stored internally as integers in the range [–1000,1000]; hence the integer (600) here and in subsequent LISP examples.

4. Except see description of metarules (Section 2.6.1.6).

5. Actually, multiple goals are possible, in which case the root of the tree might be thought of as the union of several **OR** nodes, one for each goal.

6. That is, the atom **CNTXT** in the LISP form of the rules really *is* a variable. Parameters are always constants, and values usually are.

7. Actually, questions are only asked for parameters that the system builder has indicated are "askable," as indicated by the presence of a *prompt* for the parameter.

8. In the original MYCIN implementation these were termed "lab data."

9. Allowing antecedent rules to fire whenever *any* conclusion for a parameter is made, rather than only when the parameter becomes traced, would mean that rules could suceed using "partial" values (note that this never happens with consequent rules, due to the definition of tracing), and inconsistencies could result unless extraordinary book-keeping were introduced. For example, suppose the system concludes that parameter **P** of a context is value **V** with certainty .3 and applies an antecedent rule "if **P** = **V** then **X** (.4)." If a later consequent rule concludes "**P** = **V**(–.7)," thereby making a combined certainty of **P** = **V**(–.57), what should be done about **X**? Or any rules that have fired in which **X** was used? This problem confronts sytems that have less rigidly directed control regimes; see, for example, [Trigoboff 77] and [Duda 78] for discussion of propagation of values through a semantic net. A similar problem is discussed in [Doyle 79] in connection with truth maintenance—the system has to be able to determine the assumptions on which conclusions are based, and be able to backtrack and change conclusions when an assumption is discovered to be false.

10. Except, of course, if the rule was intended to be used *only* when its premise just happened to become known by other means, in which case making it a consequent rule might cause undesired tracing.

11. Except see discussion of Unitypath (Section 2.6.2.2).

12. The inquisitive reader may have noticed at this point that antecedent rules potentially violate the statement made in Section 2.2 that once a parameter is traced, its value is known once and for all. With antecedent rules it is possible to change a parameter's value even after the parameter has been traced. The effect of this would be to make the outcome of clauses that test the parameter contingent on whether the rules in which they occur are tried before or after the firing of the antecedent rule, thereby making the order of rule evaluation and parameter tracing significant. The inconsistency resulting from the application of such an antecedent rule is undesirable.

Thus, an antecedent rule is "legal" only if it (a) fires when the parameter in its conclusion is still unknown (not yet completely traced), or (b) fires after that parameter becomes known, but makes a conclusion (with CF = 1) that is the same as the existing (traced) value of the parameter (i.e., it behaves as a no-op). Condition (a) can be guaranteed for antecedent rules whose premises are composed of **INITIALDATA** parameters and whose conclusions mention parameters of the same context (other than earlier **INITIALDATA** parameters); in particular, it is true when antecedent rules are used to prune an **INITIALDATA** list, as described in the text. Condition (b) can probably never be guaranteed; it assumes that each antecedent rule is consistent with all other rules that make conclusions about the same parameter and/or the value the client might have given for the parameter when asked earlier in the consultation. If one assumes, as EMYCIN does, that the client gives only correct answers (that are consistent with the domain model embodied in the knowledge base), then the condition is satisfied. Otherwise, the system ought to have an alarm mechanism, which would say, for example, "You gave me information *x* back in Question 10, but I have reason to believe (due to antecedent rule **R**) that *x* is false."

13. The name derives from the fact that the rule(s) involved make conclusions with CF = 1. The "path" can actually be longer than one rule. A rule's premise is "known with certainty" if for each parameter tested in the premise either (a) the parameter has already been traced and is known with certainty to be the value tested in the rule, or (b) the parameter can be deduced with certainty via a Unitypath to be the desired value (thus invoking this definition recursively).

14. This, of course, only handles one-level Unitypaths.

15. A more complete and detailed description of the predicates available in EMYCIN may be found in Appendix A.

16. Numeric parameters may also be combined arithmetically (added, subtracted, etc.), and the system can convert from one unit of measure to another to accept client input in different units from those that the program manipulates.

17. Every rule premise is already a conjunction of predicates; additionally, internal clauses (within a disjunction or mapping predicate) can be connected with **and**.

18. See Section 4.3.2 for more details regarding the definition of new predicates.

19. Contexts may also be instantiated by explicit command, much as **INITIALDATA** and **GOALS** parameters are traced explicitly; however, the mechanism is less convenient.

20. The model described in this section emerged from discussion with Dr. Shortliffe of possible ways to remedy shortcomings of the CF model observed in MYCIN; the model was subsequently incorporated into EMYCIN as well. It should be noted that the model is still very informal, but serves well for the purpose of assigning approximate measures of certainty to competing hypotheses.

21. This formula actually derives from defining CF as the likelihood ratio $P[e|h]/P[e|{\sim}h]$ $\simeq (1 - MD)/(1 - MB)$, which is in the range $[0,\infty)$, and then mapping that back into the more familiar $[-1, 1]$ range (so that $0{\to}{-}1$, $1{\to}0$, $\infty{\to}1$). For a more rigorous treatment of likelihood ratios in an inference network, see [Duda 76].

22. Rules that conclude one of the two parameters *the identity of the organism (from a culture)* and *the identity of the organisms (other than those seen on cultures or smears) that might be causing the infection* make up 40% of MYCIN's rule base.

23. *The infection that requires therapy.*

24. Actually, this last parameter might as well not be marked **ASKFIRST** at all, since the only time its rules apply is when Unitypath succeeds for them.

25. Associating a CF with a particular numeric value of a parameter would not capture the sense that values in the neighborhood of that value also have a certainty in the same neighborhood. Rules can certainly be written on a case-by-case basis to transform particular ranges of numeric data into symbolic values ("normal," "high," etc.), with appropriate certainties, as is done in the example of Chapter 3. But the ranges are still bounded by specific values, and any fuzziness in the boundaries between symbolic ranges has to be stated explicitly for each case (perhaps by assigning different certainties or different symbolic values to different parts of the range); EMYCIN provides no convenient general mechanism for manipulation of these ranges. See [Zadeh 75] for an approach that in effect assigns a probability distribution to ranges of numeric data and allows "fuzzy" statements to operate on such fuzzy sets of data in a more uniform way.

26. The system permits the client to enter CF's as part of the response to a question, but this feature has found little use to date, as it is generally viewed as the task of the system to make the judgmental conclusions, and leave the client with only "firm" data to enter.

Notes for Chapter 3

1. This is *not* a typescript of how the CLOT knowledge base was actually acquired, but rather is *based* on the original CLOT acquisition sessions after several bugs discovered during those sessions had been repaired.

2. In some cases, e.g., simple yes/no questions, the user types a single character, whereas in others the completion happens after the user types **escape** or **carriage return.**

3. On a display terminal, the system instead preloads the display editor with the suggested value, and the designer can type a carriage return to accept it, or give other commands to edit it directly, without need for the INTERLISP editor.

4. When the parameter is associated with a particular context in a consultation, the translation is the translation of the context; in the absence of a particular context (e.g., when translating a rule more generally), a generic phrase for the type of context is used.

5. When the system asks the client for such a parameter during an actual consultation, it manufactures a prompt in the "obvious" fashion by using the **TRANS**; in this case: "Is there a history of a genetic bleeding disorder in *'s family?"

6. This is not a record of a real patient, but could have been. Running a test consultation on such a small rule set may be premature—the CLOT designers actually entered over 40 rules before trying a consultation, and the case entered here does not make complete medical sense—but is done here to show some other aspects of knowledge base construction early on.

7. The consultation can be rerun with or without the printing of old questions and answers. The debugger ordinarily does without, but the default is to print them. This is necessary in this case in order that the designer be able to verify that the changes just made had the desired effect, since they concern the questions themselves.

Notes for Chapter 4

1. Appendix B lists the operators initially supplied in EMYCIN.

2. Alternatively, one could concentrate on the parameters and define rules relevant to

them ("now that you've defined the parameter, give some rules to conclude it"). In this case, one might follow a sort of "goal-directed" acquisition, acquiring first rules for the **GOALS** parameters of each context type the expert defines, and from there start working on subgoals (parameters mentioned in the rules just acquired).

3. The original version of the rule interaction checker was written by Carli Scott.

4. This is usually bad practice, however, as the rules are not independent—the more specific rule does not make sense by itself; thus some of the benefits of rule modularity are lost.

5. This situation arises principally because the **SUBJECT** combines syntactic classification (at what level in the tree will this rule be applicable) and semantic classification (what subset of syntactically legal nodes make semantic sense); this was probably a poor design choice in MYCIN. The semantic constraints would be better expressed as a separate condition or extra premise clause, leaving the **SUBJECT** as a purely syntactic guide for the rule interpreter, with which the expert need never be concerned.

6. The expert may have intended that it be applied to *all* possible contexts; however, this is not supported by the current rule interpreter. A more flexible definition of context relationships might remedy this shortcoming (see Section 6.1.2).

7. Those familiar with INTERLISP might view the Rule Checker as a form of DWIMIFY using the rule language, where ARL corresponds to CLISP, which is parsed when that format is detected as an "illegal" form.

8. **PROMPTFOR** is a function in the knowledge base editor that prompts the designer to enter the indicated property for the atom (parameter) being checked, if that property does not yet exist.

9. See Appendix A for a catalogue of the basic predicates.

10. PUFF actually uses a more sophisticated definition, allowing different degree scales and taking CF's into account; the example presented here is simply for purpose of illustration, but could have been used for initial rough testing in PUFF.

11. The parenthesized *(n)* means to translate the function's *n*th argument; the pattern *((2 1))* is a specialized form used to translate "the parameter of the context," accomplished by substituting the translation *(1)* for the asterisk in the translation *(2)*.

12. For parameters for which the designer gave a **PROMPT**, the system can generate an alternative question from the **TRANS**.

13. The **REPROMPT** property, of the same form as the **PROMPT**, is printed when the client asks for help.

14. Considered by the MYCIN designers an important consideration for the acceptance by physicians of medical consultation programs [Shortliffe 74].

15. The cases in the library are currently indexed solely by their case number, but we have plans to allow case selection based on user-specified aspects of the case (e.g., "give me all cases that have more than one positive blood culture"). A much fancier system might select relevant cases automatically based on examination of the rules recently added/modified.

16. TEIRESIAS was built as a prototype system and is not in routine use. Thus, some differences between the two systems can be attributed to the practical design consid-

erations in EMYCIN of producing a system that is efficient and convenient enough to be attractive for everyday use.

Notes for Chapter 5

1. Of course, at most one of those evaluations will require tracing a parameter, so that in the remaining evaluations only a value lookup is performed. However, once the parameter has been traced, the remaining computation performed in evaluating the clause (looking up the parameter's value and testing it according to the semantics of the predicate involved) is still repeated each time.

2. At least if the rule set grows faster than the parameter set (initial rule sets tend to be somewhat sparse and grow denser as more rules than parameters are added), since then the system overhead of tracing a parameter, asking a question, etc. stays nearly constant while more time is spent per parameter interpreting rules.

3. Also, in INTERLISP-10 the compiled version of the rules occupies far less resident space, being swappable machine code.

4. The knowledge bases to date show considerable variation in the branching factor. A rough idea can be obtained from examination of Figure 2-11 (p. 33), which showed that half of the rule sets (rules concluding about a given parameter) contain two or fewer rules (slightly more in SACON and HEADMED); such rule sets would have low branching factors a priori. Not directly evident from that table is how the larger rule sets fare. Experience with RCOMPL has shown that many rule sets have a few very common clauses for a high branching factor near the top of the tree, below which are subsets with locally high branching factors (the subsets most resembling decision tables) together with subsets of essentially unrelated rules.

5. In decision table terminology (Section 5.7.2), such a set of rules is *unambiguous*.

6. Referencing a parameter while it is being traced is prohibited (the rule fails by "circular reasoning"), except for self-referencing rules, which are handled in such a way as to satisfy this constraint if the self-referencing rules are compiled separately from the regular rules (Section 5.3.4).

7. Choosing the "most common clause" is not guaranteed to be optimal, however, either in time or space, as it makes no provision to "look ahead" to examine the possible subtrees produced by differing choices. It is easy to demonstrate cases where this choice produces a tree with more nodes than the minimum possible. For example, consider the four rules:

A and $B \Rightarrow X1$, A and $\sim B \Rightarrow X2$, B and $C \Rightarrow X3$, $\sim B$ and $C \Rightarrow X4$.

Selecting the most common clause, B, partitions the rules into two sets ($X1$, $X3$ and $X2$, $X4$), each of which has no common clauses and therefore requires an additional two nodes to test, for a total of five nodes; selecting either A or C first results in two trees of two nodes each.

Determining what choice will produce a tree that is optimal in execution time requires knowing the expected frequencies of occurrence and costs associated with each of the clauses. For example, it might pay to test a rare clause in two places if more likely clauses received better treatment. In any event, the rule interpreter's clause ordering constraint may rule out what would otherwise be the optimal clause selection.

8. Recall that this is only done for two clauses having the same context/parameter pair.

9. How RCOMPL actually makes this inference: if the branch clause is C1 = (**SAME CNTXT parm valu1**), then its negation (computed for Step 6), according to **SAME**'s **NEGATION** prop is ~C1 = (**NOTSAME CNTXT parm valu1**). RCOMPL then tests C2 = (**SAME CNTXT parm valu2**) to see if C2 $\Rightarrow$ ~C1 (so that C2 can be compiled on the false side). The answer is "yes," because by the **IMPLIES.OTHER** property, C2 $\Rightarrow$ (**DEFNOT CNTXT parm valu1**) $\Rightarrow$ ~C1 (the latter step because **DEFNOT** $\Rightarrow$ **NOTSAME**, by the **IMPLIES.FN** property of **DEFNOT**, not shown here).

10. The function **VAL1** returns the single value of a definite-valued parameter; it can be used here because **SAME** does not need to perform a match against possibly several values (competing hypotheses) for the one parameter.

11. This is analogous to eliminating free-variable lookup in deep-bound LISP. Empirically, this search up the context tree accounts for about 10% of the time spent in interpreting rules.

12. For example, in the MYCIN knowledge base fewer than 20% of the rules fall into Case (3b).

13. Recall that there may be more than one block for a single parameter if there are self-referencing rules or rules of differing **SUBJECT**'s.

14. As the author did when RCOMPL revealed some bugs in the MYCIN rule base.

15. INTERLISP fans may note an analogy with the case of editing functions that have been Block-Compiled.

16. For a description of a hashfile facility similar to the one actually used in EMYCIN, see [Teitelman 78].

17. See Appendix D for an example of the LISP code produced by RCOMPL.

18. Note that simply returning **NIL** as the value of the parameter is inadequate, since some predicates return **true** when the parameter is unknown.

19. It should also be possible, in principle, to detect the possibility of circular reasoning by a static analysis of the rule set; though the analysis is not simple (it is complicated by such things as mapping rules and context-valued parameters), it would be a useful debugging tool.

20. But this compile-time Preview has the slight advantage that it can occasionally succeed where the rule interpreter's Preview would fail due to an inability to symbolically evaluate a clause. For example, if one rule contains an "unpreviewable" clause **test** and another the clause (**NOT test**), RCOMPL knows enough to put them on opposite sides of a branch, effectively Previewing the rule on the side not taken. In one of the MYCIN cases tested (Section 5.6) a question was actually pruned away because of this.

21. For example, as noted in Section 5.6, out of 129 MYCIN cases, with an average of 65 questions per consultation, Preview pruned a total of ten questions, or a little over .01% of all the questions asked.

22. Another mitigating factor is that, although the order of the clauses within a premise is up to the whim of the system designer, rules are often written with clauses that are most likely to be known situated earlier in the premise than the ones that will invoke little-used subgoal trees—the former clauses establish the "setting" of the rule, and

the latter constitute the special considerations that make this rule distinguished. When this is the case, the rule will likely fail during normal evaluation before it gets to the clause(s) that one would want Preview to protect from tracing.

23. The first clause need not be previewed, since even if the first clause fails, it will do so before any other clause is evaluated that requires tracing. However, if the rules are such that the first clause has a high probability of being known to be false, then it might be worthwhile including it as well. Of course, if any of the clauses test information guaranteed to be already known (e.g., **INITIALDATA** parameters, as described earlier), then they can simply be moved to the front of the rule and evaluated immediately, without any of the extra "*x* is known . . ." testing.

24. Not necessarily, of course, but all other things being equal, the more frequent parameter would have had more chances to be traced by other rules already. It is interesting to note that the rule acquisition system for MYCIN described in [Shortliffe 76], written before the introduction of Preview, actually reordered clauses automatically on this basis.

25. Compiling the metarules themselves into a top-level tree, the leaves of which are alternative executions of the object-level rules, would require compiling a separate tree of object rules for each possible outcome of the metarules. That could rapidly become prohibitive, both in code space and in the time spent by RCOMPL, for even a small set of metarules.

26. A complication arises if multiple metarules for the same goal want to prune subsets of rules that overlap. These cases could only be handled if the combined effects of the metarules could be determined statically, producing a combined precondition for the rules in the overlap.

27. A simpler method, and one that would retain a greater branching factor, would be to view the static ordering as a "suggestion" that would strongly bias the selection of the branch clause at any step, but not force rules to appear in a specific order. This method could also be used to partially handle Unitypath, by behaving as though there were a metarule reading "try rules with definite conclusions (CF = 1) before rules with less than definite conclusions."

28. See note 24, chapter 2.

29. The time spent in the average PUFF consultation, 16 seconds, may be too short to provide any statistically significant result (certainly too short to gain much by compiling), but the figures are included here to illustrate the range of possible times.

30. But in the MYCIN timings, a small additional savings often occurred outside of rule execution, apparently attributable to a couple of parameters that the compiled rules avoided tracing.

31. In MYCIN, the breakdown was: 11% tracing, 4% setting up contexts, 4% in antecedent rules, and 7% in the therapy module.

32. These were cases where a rule performed a numeric computation on two or more parameters, such as "**WHENCUL+1** < **WHENSTOP**." When interpreted, all of the parameters are traced before the computation is made, but RCOMPL produces code that traces the parameters one at a time and returns **NIL** immediately when any argument is found to be unknown. The problem could be avoided in interpreted rules if EMYCIN predicates were redefined to evaluate their arguments more selectively.

33. See description of **CONCLUDET** in Appendix A.

34. If the order is truly irrelevant in *all* rules of a domain, however, the designer can set a flag to have RCOMPL ignore the clause-ordering constraint.

Notes for Chapter 6

1. The degree to which a form of representation is "unnatural" to a problem is partially subjective, depending on the ability and experience of the system designer—what is natural to one person may be difficult for another. Thus, many of the comments in this chapter regarding suitability of certain tasks are really statements of this writer's perspective regarding the suitability of those tasks.

2. There is a means by which a prior consultation can be *updated* with new information—parameter values that have changed or become known since the previous consultation. However, there is no way to write rules that examine the data from old consultations, since those data are simply replaced by the new data.

3. For one means of manipulating time-dependent parameters, see the work on the VM program [Fagan 79], which interprets real-time data from a hospital's intensive care unit.

4. MYCIN has at times during its development tried doing this without new context types by associating what would be "patient" parameters with other existing contexts, in order to have multiple values that were related in time to other known events: e.g., a parameter *the patient was febrile at the time of this culture*. This is at best a partial solution.

5. Metarules were designed for these purposes [Davis 76], but have not been used enough to test their adequacy.

6. In order to use the knowledge in an EMYCIN knowledge base for tutoring purposes in the GUIDON program [Clancey 79a], these very problems of clustering rules in the knowledge base and distinguishing such things as "contextual" clauses in rules were faced.

7. That is, the parameter of the first of two clauses, if not yet traced, will usually be asked before that of the second clause. Even this is not always guaranteed, however. If tracing the parameter in the first clause resulted in first trying rules, one of which needed the parameter in the second clause, the questions could appear in the reverse order.

8. A global metarule, applicable to any parameter being traced, could be stated as "if there are rules that use x and rules that use y, then use the former before the latter." However, that only handles the case where x and y are both traced in the course of applying rules for the same parameter. And it has no way to affect specific rules themselves that might use *both* x and y; the system designer would have to ensure that such rules were written with clauses mentioning x appearing first.

9. Except, of course, that Preview prevents a question from being asked solely to evaluate a rule that will fail outright anyway for other reasons.

10. The rule interpreter would have to stop tracing a parameter when it can see that the rules that remain for the current goal will have no appreciable effect. Specifically, it should determine what the worst possible case would be (refuting the currently strong-

est hypothesis for the parameter's value, or affirming new values), and determine if that case is significantly different from the outcome of trying *none* of the rules (i.e., stopping now), according to some threshold criterion. The knowledge base maintenance routines should help this by statically ordering the rules for a given parameter so that the likely "weightiest" ones are first. A more precise procedure would have the rule interpreter dynamically order the rules according to the particular case. These procedures might tend to ask fewer questions, at least for those knowledge bases that have many rules that make "small" inferences using additional facts that would require asking additional questions. They would, however, carry an added computational cost to the program, and would make it more difficult to compile the rules.

11. Parsing an English summary of a case is a difficult problem. Some preliminary work along these lines has been done within the framework of MYCIN [Bonnet 79].

12. However, the system designer can avoid using LISP's editor altogether if she is willing to do more typing, or is using a display on which she can use the TTYIN editor.

13. This latter dependence has been reduced by incorporating the more useful utilities into the EMYCIN executive.

14. EMYCIN *does* provide a limited "system designer profile," in the form of a collection of flags that control various aspects of the environment. For example, the designer can specify a default mode for displaying rules, or a preferred editor. Some of these flags can also be of use to a client.

15. In this mode the program uses a parameter's **TRANS**, rather than its **PROMPT**, to ask each question. This assumes that the **TRANS**, which is used to translate the parameter in rules, is terser than the **PROMPT**, whose sole role is to prompt for the parameter and can thus be written by the designer to be a little more explicit. For parameters where this is not the case, the original **PROMPT** is used after all, resulting in no change in verbosity.

16. Much of the code is swapped automatically by INTERLISP and thus uses only a fraction of its nominal size in resident space. The tables occupy more space: MYCIN's table stating the laboratory characteristics of 124 organisms alone occupies almost a fourth as much space as all the rules.

17. These were written by the author to store MYCIN's parameter translations (which use a lot of space in strings) and drug information for therapy selection.

Notes for Appendix A

1. Stated more explicitly: Each list form in a rule is considered a call to a function; the first element of the form is the function and the remaining elements are its arguments. If an argument is a list, it is evaluated in like manner, and the resulting value is passed to the function. Non-lists are taken literally, except those atoms that are designated as variables (by having the property **ALWAYSEVAL**, value **T**)—they are replaced by their values. The initial variables in EMYCIN are **CNTXT** and **TALLY**. To keep a list from being treated as a function call, it can be quoted with the LISP **QUOTE** function; to have an atom be evaluated, it must be marked as a variable or made the argument to a function that explicitly evaluates it (e.g., **LISTOF**, section A.3). NLAMBDA functions do not obey the evaluation rules above, but may evaluate their arguments in any desired fashion.

2. If a value from *valu* and a value of *parm* of *cntxt* are the same and have positive certainties cf_1 and cf_2 respectively, then the certainty of the individual match is given by $1-[cf_1-cf_2]$. In particular, this yields 1.0 if the CF's are identical, and cf_2 if $cf_1 = 1.0$.

3. The CF in the conclusion clause is multiplied by the certainty of the premise to produce a CF for the actual conclusion.

4. **PRINTCONCLUSIONS** was used in all of the CLOT examples to print the results at the end of the consultation, invoked not in the action of a rule but in accordance with the **DISPLAYRESULTS** property of the patient context.

5. This is, in fact, just **GETPROP** [*gridname, prop*].

6. The mapping functions are all **NLAMBDA** functions, as they need to evaluate their arguments selectively.

7. Or to **CAR** of the current element of *mapset* when *mapset* is a list of pairs (e.g., a call to **VAL**).

Notes for Appendix B

1. Since the parser splits apart operators and operands before it actually examines them for validity, and there is no guarantee that the operands have already been defined when the designer enters the rule, it is necessary for the parser to know a priori which embedded characters are operators. The designer can change the set of operators that are usable as parts of atom names by altering the list **DONTUNPACKCHARS**.

2. There is no way in ARL to specify the iteration variable in a mapping clause. Development of such a language device awaits an overhaul of the general context tree mechanisms.

Notes for Appendix D

1. This test is necessary because, although **SEX** is a definite-valued parameter, its value could be unknown. Thus **SEX** $\neq$ **FEMALE** does not imply **SEX** = **MALE**.

2. This test is allowed to appear "out of order" here because all of the parameters tested in this set of rules are **INITIALDATA**, hence traced before this block is invoked.

3. **ANTRY** is actually implied by **ANGROW**, but RCOMPL has no way of knowing this.

Bibliography

[Aikins 80]
Aikins, J.S. Prototypes and production rules: an approach to knowledge representation for hypothesis formation. *Proceedings of the Sixth International Joint Conference on Artificial Intelligence*, Tokyo, Japan, 1979, 1–3.

[Bennett 78]
Bennett, J.S., et al. SACON: A knowledge-based consultant for structural analysis. Computer Science Department, Stanford University, working paper HPP-78-23, September, 1978.

[Bennett 80]
Bennett, J.S., and Goldman, D. CLOT: A knowledge-based consultant for bleeding disorders. Computer Science Department, Stanford University, Memo HPP-80-7, 1980.

[Bonnet 79]
Bonnet, A. Understanding medical jargon as if it were a natural language. *Proceedings of the Sixth International Joint Conference on Artificial Intelligence*, Tokyo, Japan, 1979, 79–81.

[Buchanan 69]
Buchanan, B.G., et al. Heuristic DENDRAL: a program for generating explanatory hypotheses in organic chemistry. In *Machine Intelligence 4* (eds. B. Meltzer and D. Michie), Edinburgh University Press, 1969.

[Buchanan 78]
Buchanan, B.G., and Feigenbaum, E.A. DENDRAL and Meta-DENDRAL: their applications dimension. *Artificial Intelligence* 11:1 (1978), 5–24.

[Clancey 77]
Clancey, W.J. An antibiotic therapy selector which provides for explanations. *Proceedings of the Fifth International Joint Conference on Artificial Intelligence*, Cambridge, Massachusetts, 1977, 858.

[Clancey 79a]
Clancey, W.J. Transfer of rule-based expertise through a tutorial dialogue. Ph.D. Thesis, Computer Science Department, Stanford University, STAN-CS-769, August, 1979.

[Clancey 79b]
Clancey, W.J. and Cooper, G. Experiment: Sensitivity of MYCIN to certainty factor changes. Computer Science Department, Stanford University, Internal working paper, October, 1979.

[Davis 76]
Davis, R. Applications of meta-level knowledge to the construction, maintenance, and use of large knowledge bases. Ph.D. Thesis, Computer Science Department, Stanford University, June, 1976.

[Davis 77a]
Davis, R., Buchanan, B.G., and Shortliffe, E.H. Production rules as a representation for a knowledge-based consultation system. *Artificial Intelligence* **8**:1 (1977), 15–45.

[Davis 77b]
Davis, R. and King, J. An overview of production systems. In *Machine Intelligence 8: Machine Representations of Knowledge* (eds. E. W. Elcock and D. Michie), American Elsevier, 1977.

[Doyle 79]
Doyle, J. A glimpse of truth maintenance. *Proceedings of the Sixth International Joint Conference on Artificial Intelligence*, Tokyo, Japan, 1979, 232–237.

[Duda 76]
Duda, R.O., et al. Subjective Bayesian methods for rule-based inference systems. *AFIPS Conference Proceedings* **45**, 1976, 1075–1082.

[Duda 78]
Duda, R.O., et al. Semantic network representations in rule-based inference systems. In *Pattern-Directed Inference Systems* (eds. D. Waterman and F. Hayes-Roth), Academic Press, New York, 1978, 203–221.

[Fagan 79]
Fagan, L.M. Representation of dynamic clinical knowledge: measurement interpretation in the intensive care unit. *Proceedings of the Sixth International Joint Conference on Artificial Intelligence*, Tokyo, Japan, 1979, 260–262.

[Forgy 79a]
Forgy, C.L. On the efficient implementation of production systems. Ph.D. Thesis, Department of Computer Science, Carnegie-Mellon University, February, 1979.

[Forgy 79b]
Forgy, C.L. OPS4 User's Manual. Report CMU-CS-79-132, Department of Computer Science, Carnegie-Mellon University, July, 1979. For a brief description of an earlier implementation, see Forgy, C. and McDermott, J. OPS, a domain-independent production system, *Proceedings of the Fifth International Joint Conference on Artificial Intelligence*, Cambridge, Massachusetts, 1977, 933–939.

[Heiser 78]
Heiser, J.F., Brooks, R.E., and Ballard, J.P. Progress report: a computerized psycho-pharmacology advisor. *Proceedings of the 11th Collegium Internationale Neuro-Psycho-pharmacologicum*. Vienna, 1978.

[Hughes 68]
Hughes, M.L., Shank, R.M., and Stein, E.S. *Decision Tables*. MDI Publications, Wayne, Pennsylvania, 1968.

[King 65]
King, P.J.H. Ambiguity in limited-entry decision tables. *CACM* **8**:11 (1965), 677–681.

[Kunz 78]
Kunz, J.C., et al. A physiological rule based system for interpreting pulmonary function test results. Heuristic Programming Project, Computer Science Department, Stanford University, HPP-78-19 (Working Paper), December, 1978.

[Macsyma 74]
The MACSYMA reference manual. The MATHLAB Group, MIT, September, 1974.

[McDaniel 70]
McDaniel, H. *Decision Table Software: A Handbook*. Brandon/Systems Press, Inc., 1970.

[McDermott 78]
McDermott, J. and Forgy, C. Production system conflict resolution strategies. In *Pattern-Directed Inference Systems* (eds. D. Waterman and F. Hayes-Roth), Academic Press, New York, 1978, 177–199.

[Montalbano 62]
Montalbano, M.S. Tables, flow charts, and program logic. *IBM Systems Journal* **1** (1962), 51–63.

[Newell 72]
Newell, A. and Simon, H. *Human Problem Solving*. Prentice-Hall, 1972.

[Newell 73]
Newell, A. Production systems: models of control structures. In *Visual Information Processing* (ed. W. C. Chase), Academic Press, New York, 1973, 463–526.

[Nilsson 71]
Nilsson, N.J. *Problem Solving Methods in Artificial Intelligence*. McGraw Hill, 1971.

[Pollack 71]
Pollack, S.L. Conversion of limited-entry decision tables to computer programs. *CACM* **14**:2 (1971), 69–73.

[Pople 77]
Pople, H. The formation of composite hypotheses in diagnostic problem solving: an exercise in synthetic reasoning. *Proceedings of the Fifth International Joint Conference on Artificial Intelligence*, Cambridge, Massachusetts, 1977, 1030–1037.

[Post 43]
Post, E. Formal reductions of the general combinatorial problem. *American Journal of Math* **65** (1943), 197–268.

[Reinwald 66]
Reinwald, L.T. and Soland, R.M. Conversion of limited-entry decision tables to optimal computer programs I: minimum average processing time. *JACM* **13**:3 (1966), 339–358.

[Reinwald 67]
Reinwald, L.T. and Soland, R.M. Conversion of limited-entry decision tables to optimal computer programs II: minimum storage requirements. *JACM* **14**:4 (1967), 742–756.

[Scott 77]
Scott, A.C., et al. Explanation capabilities of knowledge-based production systems. *American Journal of Computational Linguistics*, Microfiche 62, 1977.

[Shortliffe 74]
Shortliffe, E.H., et al. Design considerations for a program to provide consultations in clinical therapeutics. *Proceedings of the 13th San Diego Biomedical Symposium*, San Diego, California, February, 1974, 311–319.

[Shortliffe 75]
Shortliffe, E.H. and Buchanan, B.G. A model of inexact reasoning in medicine. *Mathematical Biosciences* **23** (1975), 351–379.

[Shortliffe 76]
Shortliffe, E.H. *Computer-based medical consultations: MYCIN*. American Elsevier, 1976.

[Teitelman 78]
Teitelman, W. *Interlisp Reference Manual*. Xerox Palo Alto Research Center, 1978.

[Tesler 73]
Tesler, L.G., et al. The LISP70 pattern matching system. *Proceedings of the Third International Joint Conference on Artificial Intelligence*, Stanford, California, 1973, 671–676.

[Trigoboff 77]
Trigoboff, M. and Kulikowski, C.A. IRIS: a system for the propagation of inferences in a semantic net. *Proceedings of the Fifth International Joint Conference on Artificial Intelligence*, Cambridge, Massachusetts, 1977, 274–280.

[van Melle 80]
van Melle, W., et al. The EMYCIN manual. Heuristic Programming Project, Computer Science Department, Stanford University, Memo HPP-80-11 (Working Paper), 1980.

[Waterman 70]
Waterman, D.A. Generalization learning techniques for automating the learning of heuristics. *Artificial Intelligence* **1**:1 (1970), 121–170.

[Weiss 78]

Weiss, S.M., et al. A model-based method for computer-aided medical decision-making. *Artifical Intelligence* **11**:1 (1978), 145–172.

[Weiss 79]

Weiss, S.M. and Kulikowski, C.A. EXPERT: a system for developing consultation models. *Proceedings of the Sixth International Joint Conference on Artificial Intelligence*, Tokyo, Japan, 1979, 942–947.

[Yu 79a]

Yu, V.L., et al. Evaluating the performance of a computer-based consultant. *Computer Programs in Biomedicine* **9**:1 (1979), 95–102.

[Yu 79b]

Yu, V.L., et al. Antimicrobial selection by a computer: a blinded evaluation by infectious disease experts. *Journal of the American Medical Association* **242**:12 (1979), 1279–1282.

[Zadeh 75]

Zadeh, L.A. The concept of a linguistic variable and its application to approximate reasoning. *Information Sciences* **8**, pp. 199–249 (Part I); **8**, pp. 301–357 (Part II); **9**, pp. 43–80 (Part III), 1975.

Index

Page numbers in italics refer to examples in the text.